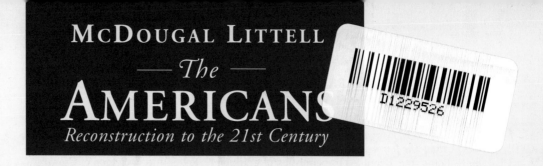

McDougal Littell
— The —
AMERICANS
Reconstruction to the 21st Century

In-Depth Resources: Unit 1

American Beginnings to 1877

McDougal Littell
A HOUGHTON MIFFLIN COMPANY
Evanston, Illinois • Boston • Dallas

Acknowledgments

CHAPTER 1

Excerpt from *The Journal of Christopher Columbus*, translated by Cecil Jane. Copyright © 1960 by Clarkson N. Potter, Inc. Reprinted by permission of Clarkson N. Potter, Inc., a division of Crown Publishers, Inc.

Excerpt from *The Memoirs of Christopher Columbus* by Stephen Marlowe. Copyright © 1987 by Stephen Marlowe. Reprinted with the permission of Scribner, a Division of Simon & Schuster, Inc.

CHAPTER 2

Excerpt from *Legacy* by James A. Michener. Copyright © 1987 by James A. Michener. Reprinted by permission of Random House, Inc.

CHAPTER 4

Excerpt from *Jubilee* by Margaret Walker Alexander. Copyright © 1966 by Margaret Walker Alexander. Reprinted by permission of Houghton Mifflin Company. All rights reserved.

ISBN-13: 978-0-618-17606-9   ISBN-10: 0-618-17606-3

Printed in the United States of America.

8 9 - BMW - 07 06

Table of Contents

CHAPTER ❷ Revolution and the Early Republic, 1763–1800

⭐ The Living Constitution

CHAPTER ❸ The Growth of a Young Nation, 1800–1850

CHAPTER ❹ The Union in Peril, 1850–1877

To the Teacher

The materials in the *In-Depth Resources* books have been carefully chosen to support and enhance the instruction given in each unit of *The Americans*. Whether you are looking for help with skill practice and reteaching or for varied enrichment opportunities, you will find the resources to target the individual needs of your students.

There are seven *In-Depth Resources* books, one for each unit of the textbook. The resources for each unit are divided by chapter and correspond to specific sections within each chapter. The Planning Guide, located in the Teacher's Edition at the beginning of each chapter, can help you plan ahead and integrate these ancillary resources into your regular instruction.

GUIDED READING

Each one-page Guided Reading worksheet is designed to help students access the information in one section of a chapter. Oriented primarily toward reading skills, the worksheets help students focus on essential aspects of a chapter section by developing their note-taking skills. As they take notes, students learn to summarize main ideas, identify cause and effect, compare and contrast, and trace the chronological sequence of events. Graphic organizers help to demonstrate these historical relationships on a visual level. In addition, the Guided Reading worksheets help students to identify the key terms and names in the section they are studying.

BUILDING VOCABULARY

Use these one-page worksheets to help students strengthen their knowledge of the significant terms and people of each chapter. The worksheets provide a variety of high-interest activities that challenge students' recall and reinforce key terms and names. Each worksheet also includes an exercise to help students practice their writing skills.

SKILLBUILDER PRACTICE

These one-page worksheets give students practice applying the specific social studies skills taught in the Skillbuilder Handbook at the back of *The Americans*. In general, each worksheet features a reading passage containing in-depth information on a topic taken from the chapter. The reading is followed by an activity that requires students to apply a specific thinking skill needed for understanding history. Use these worksheets for reinforcement or for reteaching.

RETEACHING ACTIVITY

These one-page review worksheets help students to better comprehend the main ideas of the textbook. Corresponding with each section of the book, these worksheets offer students a variety of challenging review activities that focus on the key ideas, people, and events of the history they read. Use these pages as a section quiz or as in-class activities to reinforce the main points of a chapter.

GEOGRAPHY SKILL

Use these worksheets to teach and reinforce basic map-reading skills. The eight worksheets follow a progression that begins with understanding projections; includes recognizing and using latitude, longitude, scale, and the compass rose; and concludes with interpreting legends. Each worksheet includes introductory teaching, an outline map, and questions that require students to apply the skill. Like the Geography Applications, which follow, the Geography Skills are linked to the five geographic themes: Location, Place, Movement, Region, and Human-Environment Interactions.

GEOGRAPHY APPLICATION

Use these worksheets to reinforce and practice geography skills. Each two-page worksheet includes a reading passage that deals with a topic from the chapter; a related graphic (map, chart, or graph) for students to interpret; and a page of questions about the passage and the graphic. Most of the graphics are maps—many of them combined with charts or graphs for additional information. These complex and graphically sophisticated worksheets are labeled according to the five geographic themes: Location, Place, Movement, Region, and Human-Environment Interaction.

OUTLINE MAP

A one-page outline map and a page of related questions are included in each *In-Depth Resources* book. These worksheets can be given to students who have difficulty with fundamental map skills. The outline map serves as the sole basis for the accompanying page of questions; students need not turn back to the pupil edition. Use the Outline Map worksheets for reteaching and remediation.

PRIMARY SOURCES

Because primary sources both enrich and enliven the study of history, they are invaluable in any classroom. The four pages of primary sources collected for each chapter were chosen to stimulate as well as inform. Included are items that add dimension to a historical period—such as artifacts, political cartoons, and facsimile pages—as well as important historical documents. Moreover, in keeping with the emphasis on individual experience throughout *The Americans*, the primary sources also include diary entries, personal letters, and eyewitness accounts of important events. The impact of these documents and artifacts is enhanced by activities that invite students to participate in history through discussion, research, and short projects.

The primary sources in the *In-Depth Resources* books are one- or two-page selections intended for use in short time periods or as homework. For longer selections, see the *Electronic Library of Primary Sources* available on CD-ROM. The Teacher's Resource Book for the *American Stories* video series also includes primary sources and extension activities.

LITERATURE SELECTIONS

Literature engages the heart and the imagination. When combined with the study of history, it gives students the opportunity to feel the pulse of the past. The literature selections in the *In-Depth Resources* books have been chosen with the goal of bringing history alive. Excerpts are long enough (about three pages) for students to have a sustained imaginative experience. Use the selections as gateways into history for students of all ability levels.

AMERICAN LIVES

These biographical sketches of the prominent and the not-so-prominent are provided to bring a human dimension to the vast array of historical figures presented in *The Americans*. There are two one-page biographies for each chapter.

As a study aid to students whose first language is Spanish, the following worksheets from the *In-Depth Resources* have been translated and can be found in the book titled *Access for Students Acquiring English: Spanish Translations*.

- Guided Reading
- Outline Map
- Skillbuilder Practice
- Projects for Citizenship
- Geography Application
- Thematic Review Activities

Name _____ Date _____

GEOGRAPHY SKILLS   Understanding Projections
GEOGRAPHICAL THEME: LOCATION

Because the earth is a sphere, the best model of the earth is a **globe.** On a globe, each continent and ocean can be shown proportionally—the correct size and at correct distance, in the correct direction, from the others. On flat surfaces, however, the curved surface of the earth must be mapped as though it were flat. To do this, mapmakers use a variety of **projections.**

A projection is a technique for giving each location on the earth a corresponding place on a flat surface. All projections distort the earth to some degree. That is why features of the earth look different on different kinds of maps. For instance, areas farthest from the equator, such as Greenland and Antarctica, sometimes appear "stretched." Look at the four common projections shown below and answer the questions.

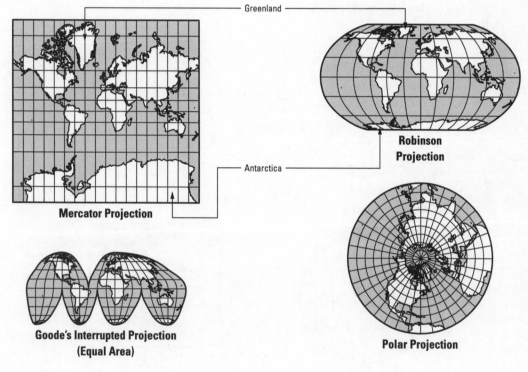

Greenland

Antarctica

Mercator Projection

Robinson Projection

Goode's Interrupted Projection (Equal Area)

Polar Projection

1. Which of the four projections shows only half of the world? _____

2. Compare the sizes of Greenland and Antarctica on the Mercator projection with the Robinson projection. _____

3. What would you consider the main drawback of Goode's Interrupted projection? _____

_____

4. Why do you think that the Mercator projection is considered the best for plotting direction?

_____

Name _____   Date _____

Most maps contain imaginary horizontal and vertical lines of measurement. Horizontal lines, running east and west, are called **latitude lines** or parallels. Vertical lines, running north and south, are called **longitude lines** or meridians. The lines are numbered in degrees (shown by the symbol °).

Latitude starts at 0°, known as the equator, where the earth is at its widest. There are 90 degrees north of the equator and 90 degrees south

of it. Longitude starts at 0°, the Prime Meridian, and goes 180 degrees west and 180 degrees east.

Because latitude and longitude cross and form a grid, the use of these lines to locate places is called the grid system. Every place in the world has a single grid location—where its latitude and longitude intersect. Study the maps below and answer the questions.

Latitude Lines (Parallels)

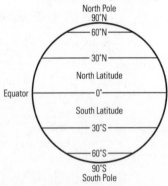

Longitude Lines (Meridians)

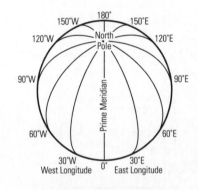

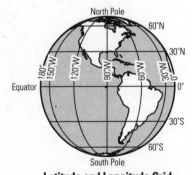

Latitude and Longitude Grid

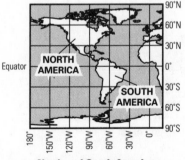

North and South America

1. Find the Prime Meridian. What are the three continents through which it passes? _____

_____

2. How many degrees separate the North Pole from the South Pole? _____

3. An airplane disappears from radar at 60° W and 30° S. Over which continent was it flying?

_____

4. A ship signals distress from 45° S and 120° W. Mark the map titled "North and South America" at the approximate point where a ship might be found.

2 Geography Skills

Name _____   Date _____

GEOGRAPHY SKILLS

Recognizing Continents and Oceans

GEOGRAPHICAL THEME: REGION

The largest land masses on earth are called **continents.** Two of these continents—Australia and Antarctica—are not connected to other land masses. The continents of North and South America are connected to each other by a narrow piece of land called an isthmus. Europe and Asia, however, share one large land mass. The line that divides them is not as well defined as the borders defining the other continents.

Most of the earth—71 percent of its surface—is covered by salt water. Large sections of this body of water are called **oceans.** The four main oceans are the Atlantic, Pacific, Arctic, and Indian Oceans. Smaller bodies of water are called **seas,** as in the South China Sea and Arabian Sea. Study the map below and answer the questions.

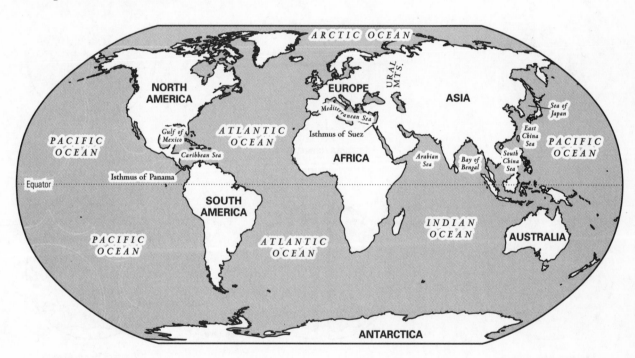

1. What are the seven continents? _____

_____

2. Where is most of the earth's land mass—north or south of the equator? _____

3. Which ocean would you cross traveling from Australia to Africa? _____

4. What sea lies between Africa and Europe? _____

Name _____ Date _____

Mapmakers sometimes draw the earth as though they were seeing it from high above the North Pole, the South Pole, or the equator. When they do this, they show only one-half of the earth's surface, or one **hemisphere.** The word comes from *hemi,* meaning half, and *sphere,* meaning ball or globe.

Four hemispheres are typically used on maps—the Northern, Southern, Western, and Eastern Hemispheres. These hemispheres are shown below.

Northern Hemisphere

Northern Hemisphere

Southern Hemisphere

Southern Hemisphere

Western Hemisphere

Western Hemisphere

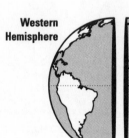

Eastern Hemisphere

Eastern Hemisphere

1. What geographical line separates the Northern and Southern Hemispheres? _____

2. What two hemispheres are separated by an imaginary line that runs north and south through the Atlantic Ocean ? _____

3. Which continents lie mostly or completely in the Northern Hemisphere? _____

_____

4. Which two continents lie partly in the Western Hemisphere and partly in the Eastern Hemisphere?

_____

4 Geography Skills

Name _____ Date _____

5 GEOGRAPHY SKILLS   Reading Physical Maps
GEOGRAPHICAL THEME: PLACE

Physical maps represent the large natural features of a place. They show **landforms,** such as mountains and plains, and **bodies of water,** such as rivers and lakes. Some physical maps show the distribution of climate or vegetation.

Below is a physical map showing major landforms in the United States. These landforms vary in **elevation** or relief, meaning height above sea level. Study this map carefully, and answer the questions that follow.

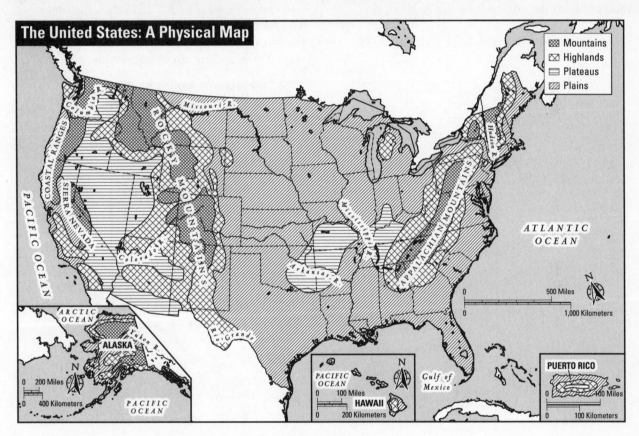

1. What four types of landforms does this map represent?_____

2. Which landform does **not** appear in Alaska? _____

_____

3. Which region of the United states has no mountains? _____

4. Based on the map, in which direction would you expect each of the following rivers to flow: the Missouri River, the Colorado River, the Rio Grande?_____

_____

Name _____ Date _____

6 GEOGRAPHY SKILLS Using Scales and
the Compass Rose

GEOGRAPHICAL THEME: MOVEMENT

The **scale** of a map helps you determine the actual size or length of any features or of any distance between two points. It is a ratio between a unit of length on a map and a unit of distance on the earth. Typically, a scale shows a length of line and indicates the number of miles or kilometers that length represents on the map. A map that covers 1,000 miles in one inch has a scale of 1:1,000.

The compass rose is a pointed symbol that shows a map's orientation on the globe. It is usually placed on an area of the map near one edge, away from map details that could make the device difficult to find. On maps showing both water and land, the compass rose is usually placed on the water. The compass rose may show all four cardinal directions—N, S, E, W—or just one, north. Study the maps below and answer the questions.

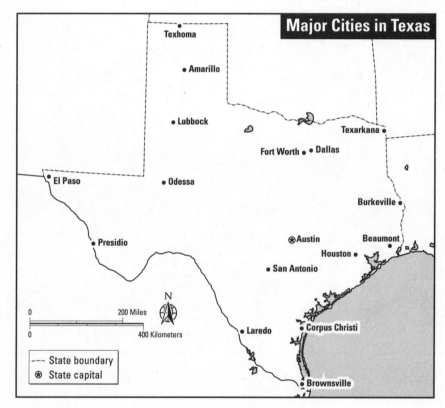

1. How many miles are shown on the scale? How many kilometers?_____

2. About how many miles is Odessa from Forth Worth? How many kilometers? _____

3. In what direction would you travel to reach Texhoma from Odessa?_____

4. In what direction would you travel to reach Presidio from El Paso? _____

Name _____   Date _____

7 GEOGRAPHY SKILLS Interpreting Lines, Labels, and Symbols

GEOGRAPHICAL THEME: HUMAN-ENVIRONMENT INTERACTION

Maps show more than just size and direction. They also define borders of cities, regions, states, and countries. They can be used to depict historical events, to demonstrate how geography has influenced history, and to illustrate human interaction with the environment.

Such information found on a map comes from a reading of its various lines, labels, and symbols. **Lines** of various widths indicate land boundaries, types of roads and waterways, and routes of movement. **Labels** are words on a map that identify such things as cities, states, countries, continents, and bodies of water. **Symbols** are decorative objects such as large circles, dots, stars, and bursts used to identify an area's special features—cities, battle sites, resources, and the like. Study the map below and answer the questions.

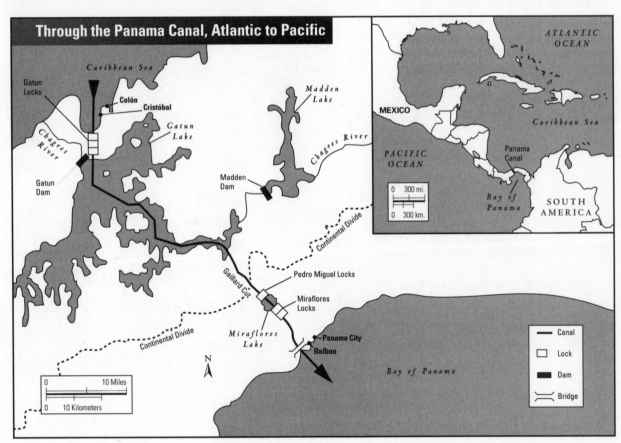

1. What locks do you see on the map? _____

2. What dams do you see?_____

3. What two bodies of water does the canal connect?_____

4. What direction does a ship travel through the canal from Colón to Balboa?_____

Geography Skills 7

Name _____ Date _____

GEOGRAPHY SKILLS   Understanding Legends (Keys)
GEOGRAPHICAL THEME: HUMAN-ENVIRONMENT INTERACTION

The lines and symbols that appear on a map often need further explanation. For this reason, a legend, also known as a key, is often used. A **legend** is a small table within a map that explains what some symbols and lines mean.

A legend is also used to indicate the meaning of any colored areas on a map. For black-and-white maps, patterns such as diagonal lines, large and small dot fields, and cross-hatching are commonly used to show separate regions within a particular boundary. The legend reproduces a sampling of the pattern or color and then identifies what it stands for. Study the map and answer the questions.

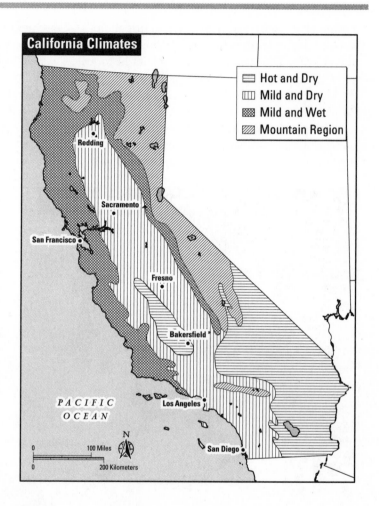

1. What are the four main weather patterns represented in the legend? _____

_____

2. Which parts of California are the driest? _____

3. Which parts of California probably receive the most precipitation (rain or snow)? _____

_____

4. What is the main difference between the climate of San Francisco and the climate of Los Angeles,

according to this map? _____

8 Geography Skills

Name _____ Date _____

REVIEW CHAPTER **1**
Section 1

GUIDED READING *The Americas, West Africa, and Europe*

A. As you read about the cultures of the Americas, West Africa, and Europe, fill out the chart below by writing notes that describe the achievements of those cultures.

	Achievements
1. Ancient Americans	
2. Native Americans	
3. West Africans	
4. Europeans	

B. On the back of this paper, define and explain the significance of the following:

Beringia land bridge	Anasazi	Pueblo
Songhai	Reformation	caravel

Name _____ Date _____

REVIEW CHAPTER 1

Section 2

GUIDED READING *Spanish North America*

A. As you read this section, fill out the chart below to help you better understand the motivations and consequences of European exploration and colonization in the Americas.

Columbus's Exploration of the Americas

Motivations	Methods
1. Why did Columbus come to the Americas?	2. How did European contact change the Americas?

Conquistadors' Conquest of Central and North America

Motivations	Methods
3. What motivated Spain's conquest?	4. How were the Spanish able to succeed?

Spanish Establishment of Missions

Motivations	Results
5. Why did the missionaries come to North America?	6. What resulted from the spread of missions?

B. On the back of this paper, identify or define each of the following:

| conquistadors | Hernándo Cortés | mestizo | *encomienda* |
| Columbian Exchange | Taino | Popé | |

Name _____ Date _____

GUIDED READING *Early British Colonies*

As you read about Jamestown, the Massachusetts Bay Colony, New Netherland, and Pennsylvania, fill out the chart below by writing notes that describe aspects of each colony.

JAMESTOWN	
1. Settlers	2. Leaders
3. Motives for Settlement	4. Relations with Native Americans

MASSACHUSETTS BAY	
5. Settlers	6. Leaders
7. Motives for Settlement	8. Relations with Native Americans

NEW NETHERLAND	
9. Settlers	10. Motives for Settlement
11. Relations with Native Americans	12. Relations with England

PENNSYLVANIA	
13. Settlers	14. Leaders
15. Motives for Settlement	16. Relations with Native Americans

GUIDED READING *The Colonies Come of Age*

A. As you read this section, fill out the chart below with some different characteristics
of the Northern and Southern colonies.

Northern Colonies	Southern Colonies

B. Fill out this chart by comparing the Enlightenment and the Great Awakening.

	The Enlightenment	The Great Awakening
1. What kind of movement was it (intellectual, social, political, religious)?		
2. Who were its key figures in the colonies?		
3. What ideas did it stress?		
4. What did it encourage people to do?		

REVIEW CHAPTER 1   **BUILDING VOCABULARY** *Exploration and the Colonial Era*

A. Matching Write the letter of the term or name on the line that best matches its description.

a. joint-stock companies   f. Islam
b. Hernándo Cortés   g. mercantilism
c. Treaty of Tordesillas   h. French and Indian War
d. middle passage   i. Pueblo
e. Reformation   j. encomienda

_____ 1. descendants of the Anasazi and Hohokam

_____ 2. founded in Arabia in 622 by the prophet Muhammad

_____ 3. movement that challenged church practices and papal authority

_____ 4. Spanish explorer who defeated the Aztec

_____ 5. agreement between Spain and Portugal over division of Western Hemisphere

_____ 6. system by which Spanish colonists forced Native Americans to work for them

_____ 7. groups of investors who pool their money to support establishment of a colony

_____ 8. economic system that encouraged the establishment of colonies

_____ 9. leg of the triangular trade that brought Africans to the Americas for slavery

_____ 10. conflict between France and England for control of North America

B. Completion Select the term or name that best completes the sentence.

Islam   Reformation   Renaissance
Christianity   Columbian Exchange   John Winthrop
John Smith   Proclamation of 1763   Great Awakening

1. _____ is a religion based on the teachings of Jesus.

2. By encouraging people to seek adventure and discovery, the _____ helped to fuel European exploration.

3. The _____ brought new goods back and forth between the eastern and western hemispheres.

4. _____ called on his fellow colonists to build a "City Upon a Hill."

5. In the wake of the French and Indian War, the _____ angered colonists seeking to move westward.

B. Writing Imagine you are a colonist writing to a relative in Europe about the dramatic cultural changes taking place in the colonies during the early and mid-1700s. Describe these changes in a paragraph using the following terms.

Enlightenment   **Benjamin Franklin**   **Great Awakening**   **Jonathan Edwards**

SKILLBUILDER PRACTICE *Interpreting Maps*

The North American continent in the 1400s was rich with Native American cultures. The map on page 7 of your textbook provides information about the names of the peoples, where they lived, and with whom they traded. To learn as much as you can from this map, study the legend, the compass rose, and the scale of the map. Then answer the questions below. (See Skillbuilder Handbook, p. R25.)

1. What region did the Pawnee live in? _____

   How do you know? _____

   _____

2. Name two nations that probably traded with the Cherokee.

   _____

3. What peoples inhabited the area that became California?

   _____

4. Locate the easternmost trade route, which runs from the southern tip of what is

   now Florida north to the Wampanoag territory. How long, in miles, was this route? _____

   How did you measure the distance? _____

   _____

5. Name three groups shown on the map that lived outside the present-day boundaries of the United

   States.

   _____

6. If the Zuni had followed a major trade route, how far, in miles, would they have

   traveled to get to the Pacific coast?_____

7. What direction and about how far would Chinook people have traveled to get to

   Arapaho country?_____

   Do you think it's likely that the Chinook would have traveled there? Why or
   why not?

   _____

   _____

   _____

REVIEW CHAPTER
1
Section 2

SKILLBUILDER PRACTICE *Using the Internet*

From the voyages of Columbus to the establishment of New Spain, the section entitled "Spanish North America" is filled with topics that appear on numerous web sites on the Internet. Below are the steps one takes to find and analyze a page on the McDougal Littell Web site pertaining to the Spanish exploratioon of Florida. Use these steps to locate and analyze a Web page about a topic in Section 2 that interests you. Then answer the questions at the bottom of the page. (See Skillbuilder Handbook, p. R29.)

1. Log on to the Internet. Then click on a search engine, such as *Yahoo!*, *Excite*, *Lycos*, or *WebCrawler*, and type in the name *McDougal Littell*.

2. When the McDougal Littell address appears, click on it.

3. In the menu at the botom of the McDougal Littell home page, click on *Social Studies*.

4. In the column on the left side of the Social Studies page, click on *U.S. History Textbook Resources*.

5. Click on the icon *The Americans*.

6. In the bottom area of the ClassZone page move the scroll bar to *Chapter 2*. Then click on *Links*.

7. Move to the center of the page and click on *Florida of the Conquistador*.

8. Read the page's information about the various conquistadors who explored Florida.

1. Now write a brief interpretation of the picture, telling who you think is fighting whom.

_____

_____

_____

_____

_____

_____

2. Explain how the historical information helped you interpret the picture.

_____

_____

_____

_____

_____

_____

SKILLBUILDER PRACTICE *Visual Sources*

One picture or visual source doesn't always tell the whole story. Look at the two pictures of Colonial urban life on page 34 of your textbook. Then fill in the Venn diagram with similarities and differences between the two pictures and answer the questions that follow. (See Skillbuilder Handbook, p. R23.)

Differences   **Similarities**   **Differences**

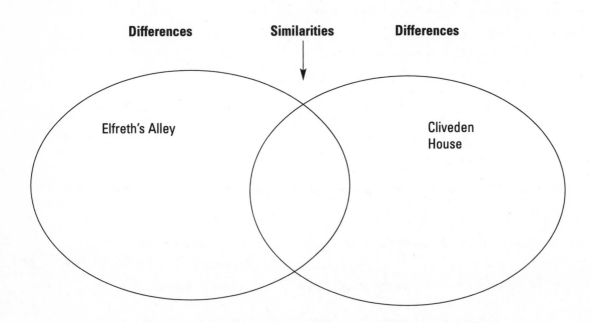

Elfreth's Alley

Cliveden
House

1. What do you think is the most important difference between the two residences?

   _____

   _____

2. Which, if either, picture do you think is the more accurate depiction of urban life in

   the Colonies? Explain your opinion.

   _____

   _____

   _____

3. What other historical sources would you look for to find out more about daily urban life

   in Colonial times? _____

   _____

   _____

REVIEW CHAPTER 1

Section 1

RETEACHING ACTIVITY *The Americas, West Africa, and Europe*

Evaluating

Write *T* in the blank if the statement is true. If the statement is false, write *F* in the blank and then write the corrected statement on the line below.

_____ 1. The Pueblo settled in the valley of Mexico during the 1200s and developed a thriving and sophisticated civilization.

_____

_____ 2. Native Americans believed that land was for sharing and that no one could own it.

_____

_____ 3. The kingdoms of Africa had had little contact with the outside world on the eve of European exploration.

_____

_____ 4. European society in the 1400s was based on a strict social hierarchy, and few people rose above the social position of their birth.

_____

_____ 5. The Crusades was a series of military expeditions to convert all Native Americans to Christianity.

_____

_____ 6. The four major nations that emerged in Europe during the 1400s were Portugal, Spain, France, and Germany.

_____

_____ 7. European monarchs supported overseas exploration because they needed to find new sources of wealth to support their growing armies and administrative bureaucracies.

_____

_____ 8. The English led the way for European exploration by first rounding the southern tip of Africa and later reaching India.

_____

RETEACHING ACTIVITY *Spanish North America*

Sequencing

A. Put the events below in the correct chronological order using the letters *A* through *H*.

_____ 1. Pueblo leader Popé leads a rebellion against Spanish missionaries.

_____ 2. Spaniard Francisco Pizzaro conquers the Inca.

_____ 3. Spain and Portugal sign the Treaty of Tordesillas.

_____ 4. Spanish conquistador Hernándo Cortés defeats the Aztec.

_____ 5. Christopher Columbus reaches the Americas.

_____ 6. The Spanish establish the outpost of St. Augustine on the Florida coast.

_____ 7. Navigator Juan Rodriguez Cabrillo explores modern-day San Diego.

_____ 8. England defeats the Spanish Armada.

Matching

B. Match the following explorers with country or countries for which they sailed.

France   England

   Spain   Netherlands

_____ 1. Henry Hudson

_____ 2. Giovanni da Verrazzano

_____ 3. Jacques Cartier

_____ 4. John Cabot

_____ 5. Francisco Vásquez de Coronado

_____ 6. Robert Cavelier Siuer de LaSalle

Name _____ Date _____

Reading Comprehension

Choose the best answer for each item. Write the letter of your answer in the blank.

_____ 1. The Jamestown settlement was saved in large part by the development of the highly profitable crop
   a. indigo.
   b. rice.
   c. tobacco.

_____ 2. The first representative body in colonial America was the
   a. House of Burgesses.
   b. Mayflower Compact.
   c. Continental Congress.

_____ 3. Bacon's Rebellion involved an uprising by the frontier colonists of
   a. Massachusetts.
   b. Virginia.
   c. Georgia.

_____ 4. The Puritan dissenter who claimed that worshippers did not need the church to help them interpret the Bible was
   a. Anne Hutchinson.
   b. Roger Williams.
   c. John Winthrop.

_____ 5. Disputes between Puritans and Native Americans arose mainly over land and
   a. gold.
   b. taxes.
   c. religion.

_____ 6. The Dutch colony of New Netherland along the Atlantic Coast of North America was eventually taken over by the
   a. English.
   b. Spanish.
   c. French.

_____ 7. One colonial industry that benefited greatly from the Navigation Acts was
   a. ironworks.
   b. shipbuilding.
   c. agriculture.

_____ 8. The colonial assemblies were elected by
   a. the English Parliament.
   b. all of the colony's adults.
   c. the colony's landowning white males.

Name _____ Date _____

REVIEW CHAPTER **1** Section 4

RETEACHING ACTIVITY *The Colonies Come of Age*

Outlining

Below is a partial outline of events related to the growth the American colonies. Complete the outline by adding supporting details for each heading.

I. A Plantation Economy Arises in the South

    A._____

    B. _____

    C._____

II. Commerce Grows in the North

    A. _____

    B. _____

    C. _____

III. The Enlightenment

    A. _____

    B. _____

IV. The Great Awakening

    A. _____

    B. _____

V. The French and Indian War

    A. _____

    B._____

    C._____

REVIEW CHAPTER 1

Section 4

GEOGRAPHY APPLICATION: MOVEMENT *The Triangular Trade*

Directions: Read the paragraphs below and study the map and pie graphs carefully. Then answer the questions that follow.

A trade route known as the triangular trade developed among the American colonies, Africa, and the West Indies. Over a period of 200 years, the middle passage of the triangular trade brought millions of Africans to work as slaves in the Americas.

The vast majority of slaves brought to North America were bound for plantations in the Southern colonies. However, the Northern colonies also played a major part in this pattern. Manufacturers there turned West Indian sugar and molasses into rum. Some of this rum then was sent to Africa as the first leg of the triangular trade and was used to buy slaves.

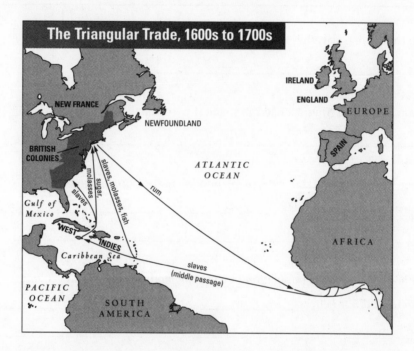

The Triangular Trade, 1600s to 1700s

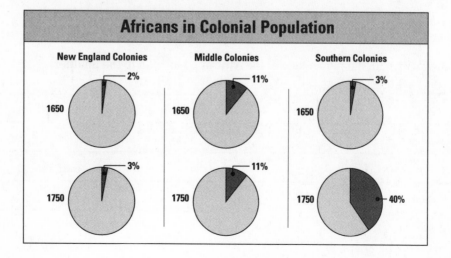

Africans in Colonial Population

New England Colonies — 1650: 2%, 1750: 3%

Middle Colonies — 1650: 11%, 1750: 11%

Southern Colonies — 1650: 3%, 1750: 40%

Exploration and the Colonial Era 21

Interpreting Text and Visuals

1. Why was the trade route of rum, slaves, and sugar and molasses called the
   Triangular Trade? _____

   _____

2. Of what did the middle passage consist? _____

   _____

3. What were the destinations of the African slaves? _____

   _____

   Why do you think some slaves were kept in the West Indies? _____

   _____

4. Which section of colonial America had the smallest percentage of Africans in 1750? _____

   _____

5. Which section of the colonies showed a huge increase in the percentage of its
   African population in about 1750? _____

   _____

6. What happened to the African population in New England and the Middle colonies
   between 1650 and 1750? Why? _____

   _____

   _____

   _____

7. Explain the increase in the percentage of the African population in the Southern
   colonies during the years shown. _____

   _____

   _____

   _____

   _____

Name _____ Date _____

REVIEW CHAPTER

1

Section 2

OUTLINE MAP *Spain Explores North America*

A. Review the map of European Exploration on textbook page 15. Then label the
following bodies of water, land areas, islands, and routes of Spanish explorers on
the accompanying outline map.

Bodies of Water	Land Areas and Cities	Routes of Explorers
Pacific Ocean	North America	De Soto
Atlantic Ocean	Mexico	Cabrillo
Gulf of Mexico	Cuba	Coronado
Mississippi River	Hispaniola	Cabeza de Vaca
Caribbean Sea	Santa Fe	Ponce de León
	Tenochtitlán	Cortés

B. After completing the map, use it to answer the following questions.

1. Which Spanish explorer sailed around the coast of Florida? _____

2. Which explorer reached as far inland as present-day Kansas? _____

    About many miles did he cover to reach central Kansas? _____

3. Which explorer crossed the Mississippi River? _____

4. Describe the route of Cabeza de Vaca from the Gulf of Mexico to Tenochtitlán
    (Mexico City). _____

    _____

    _____

5. Which Spanish explorers traveled mainly by water? _____

6. The routes of which two explorers began from present-day Cuba? _____

7. Through which present-day states did each of the following explorers travel?
    (If necessary, use the United States political map in the Atlas of your textbook.)

    a. De Soto _____

    _____

    b. Coronado _____

    _____

Exploration and the Colonial Era 23

Spanish Explorers in the 1500s

PRIMARY SOURCE *from* The Iroquois Constitution

In the 15th century, five separate nations of Iroquois—Mohawk, Seneca, Cayuga, Oneida, and Onondaga—united to form the League of Five Nations. The purpose of the Iroquois League was to end internal warfare and to form a strong alliance against outside enemies. To further their goals, the league created a constitution, called the Great Binding Law, that consisted of 117 individual laws and customs governing all aspects of life—from self-government and war to family relationships, religion, symbolism, and burial rites. In the following excerpt, the speaker Dekanawidah is the great Mohawk leader credited with establishing the Great Peace among the nations. He speaks to Adodarhoh, leader of the Onondaga. In this English translation, the term Lord means "chief."

1 I am Dekanawidah and with the Five Nations' Confederate Lords I plant the Tree of the Great Peace. I plant it in your territory, Adodarhoh, and the Onondaga Nation, in the territory of you who are Firekeepers.

I name the tree the Tree of the Great Long Leaves. Under the shade of this Tree of the Great Peace we spread the soft white feathery down of the globe thistle as seats for you, Adodarhoh, and your cousin Lords.

We place you upon those seats, spread soft with the feathery down of the globe thistle, there beneath the shade of the spreading branches of the Tree of Peace. There shall you sit and watch the Council Fire of the Confederacy of the Five Nations, and all the affairs of the Five Nations shall be transacted at this place before you, Adodarhoh, and your cousin Lords, by the Confederate Lords of the Five Nations.

2 Roots have spread out from the Tree of the Great Peace, one to the north, one to the east, one to the south and one to the west. The name of these roots is The Great White Roots and their nature is Peace and Strength.

If any man or any nation outside the Five Nations shall obey the laws of the Great Peace and make known their disposition to the Lords of the Confederacy, they may trace the Roots to the Tree and if their minds are clean and they are obedient and promise to obey the wishes of the Confederate Council, they shall be welcomed to take shelter beneath the Tree of the Long Leaves.

We place at the top of the Tree of the Long Leaves an Eagle who is able to see afar. If he sees in the distance any evil approaching or any danger threatening he will at once warn the people of the Confederacy. . . .

6 I, Dekanawidah, appoint the Mohawk Lords the heads and the leaders of the Five Nations

Confederacy. The Mohawk Lords are the foundation of the Great Peace and it shall, therefore, be against the Great Binding Law to pass measures in the Confederate Council after the Mohawk Lords have protested against them.

No council of the Confederate Lords shall be legal unless all the Mohawk Lords are present. . . .

9 All the business of the Five Nations Confederate Council shall be conducted by the two combined bodies of Confederate Lords. First the question shall be passed upon by the Mohawk and Seneca Lords, then it shall be discussed and passed by the Oneida and Cayuga Lords. Their decisions shall then be referred to the Onondaga Lords (Firekeepers) for final judgment.

The same process shall obtain when a question is brought before the council by an individual or a War Chief.

from Arthur C. Parker, *The Constitution of the Five Nations or the Iroquois Book of the Great Law* (New York State Museum *Bulletin*). Reprinted in William N. Fenton, ed., *Parker on the Iroquois* (Syracuse, N. Y.: Syracuse University Press, 1968), 30–60.

Discussion Questions

1. The Tree of the Great Peace has both literal and figurative meanings. Discuss some of the things it might symbolize to the Iroquois.
2. What advantages do you think the Iroquois gained by establishing the constitution? What disadvantages, if any, might there have been?
3. Some historians claim that the Iroquois constitution had an influence on the U.S. Constitution. Look briefly at the beginning of the U.S. Constitution on pages 84–85 in your textbook and discuss some similarities and differences between the two constitutions.

REVIEW CHAPTER

1

Section 2

PRIMARY SOURCE *from* **The Journal of Christopher Columbus**

Columbus kept a ship's log, or journal, of his historic voyage. When he returned to Spain in 1493, he presented the journal to King Ferdinand and Queen Isabella. The version printed here was originally copied by the missionary Bartolomé de Las Casas and refers to Columbus in the third person as "the admiral" unless quoting him directly. As you read, think about the reactions of Columbus, his crew, and the Taino when they first encountered one another.

THURSDAY, OCTOBER 11th / . . . Two hours after midnight land appeared, at a distance of about two leagues from them. They took in all sail, remaining with the mainsail, which is the great sail without bonnets, and kept jogging, waiting for day, a Friday, on which they reached a small island of the Lucayos, which is called in the language of the Indians "Guanahaní." Immediately they saw naked people, and the admiral went ashore in the armed boat, and Martin Alonso Pinzón and Vicente Yañez, his brother, who was captain of the Niña. The admiral brought out the royal standard, and the captains went with two banners of the Green Cross, which the admiral flew on all the ships as a flag, with an F [for Ferdinand] and a Y [for Isabella], and over each letter their crown, one being on one side of the ✠ and the other on the other. When they had landed, they saw very green trees and much water and fruit of various kinds. The admiral called the two captains and the others who had landed, and Rodrigo de Escobedo, secretary of the whole fleet, and Rodrigo Sanchez de Segovia, and said that they should bear witness and testimony how he, before them all, took possession of the island, as in fact he did, for the King and Queen, his Sovereigns, making the declarations which are required, as is contained more at length in the testimonies which were there made in writing. Soon many people of the island gathered there. What follows are the actual words of the admiral, in his book of his first voyage and discovery of these Indies.

"I," he says, "in order that they might feel great amity towards us, because I knew that they were a people to be delivered and converted to our holy faith rather by love than by force, gave to some among them some red caps and some glass beads, which they hung round their necks, and many other things of little value. At this they were greatly pleased and became so entirely our friends that it was a wonder to see. Afterwards they came swimming to the ships' boats, where we were, and brought us parrots and cotton thread in balls, and spears and many other things, and we exchanged for them other things, such as small glass beads and hawks' bells, which we gave to them. In fact, they took all and gave all, such as they had, with good will, but it seemed to me that they were a people very deficient in everything. They all go naked as their mother bore them, and the women also, although I saw only one very young girl. And all those whom I did see were youths, so that I did not see one who was over thirty years of age; they were very well built, with very handsome bodies and very good faces. Their hair is coarse almost like the hairs of a horse's tail and short; they wear their hair down over their eyebrows, except for a few strands behind, which they wear long and never cut. Some of them are painted black, and they are the colour of the people of the Canaries, neither black nor white, and some of them are painted white and some red and some in any colour that they find. Some of them paint their faces, some their whole bodies, some only the eyes, and some only the nose. They do not bear arms or know them, for I showed to them swords and they took them by the blade and cut themselves through ignorance. They have no iron. Their spears are certain reeds, without iron, and some of these have a fish tooth at the end, while others are pointed in various ways. They are all generally fairly tall, good looking and well proportioned. I saw some who bore marks of wounds on their bodies, and I made signs to them to ask how this came about, and they indicated to me that people came from other islands, which are near, and wished to capture them, and they defended themselves. And I believed and still believe that they come here from the mainland to take them for slaves. They should be good servants and of quick intelligence, since I see that they very soon say all that is said to them, and I believe that they would easily be made Christians, for it appeared to me that they had no creed. Our Lord willing, at the time of my departure I will bring back six of them to Your Highnesses, that they may learn to talk. I saw no beast of any kind in this island, except parrots." All these are the words of the admiral.

SATURDAY, OCTOBER 13th / As soon as day broke, there came to the shore many of these men, all youths, as I have said, and all of a good height, very handsome people. Their hair is not curly, but loose and coarse as the hair of a horse; all have very broad foreheads and heads, more so than has any people that I have seen up to now. Their eyes are very lovely and not small. They are not at all black, but the colour of Canarians, and nothing else could be expected, since this is in one line from east to west with the island of Hierro in the Canaries. Their legs are very straight, all alike; they have no bellies but very good figures. They came to the ship in boats, which are made of a treetrunk like long boat and all of one piece. They are very wonderfully carved, considering the country, and large, so that in some forty or forty-five men came. Others are smaller, so that in some only a solitary man came. They row them with a paddle, like a baker's peel, and they travel wonderfully fast. If one capsizes, all at once begin to swim and right it, baling it out with gourds which they carry with them. They brought balls of spun cotton and parrots and spears and other trifles, which it would be tedious to write down, and they gave all for anything that was given to them. And I was attentive and laboured to know if they had gold, and I saw that some of them wore a small piece hanging from a hole which they have in the nose, and from signs I was able to understand that, going to the south or going round the island to the south, there was a king who had large vessels of it and possessed much gold. I endeavoured to make them go there, and afterwards saw that they were not inclined for the journey. I resolved to wait until the afternoon of the following day, and after that to leave for the south-west, for, as many of them indicated to me, they said that there was land to the south and to the south-west and to the north-west, and that those of the north-west often came to attack them. So I resolved to go to the south-west, to seek the gold and precious stones. This island is fairly large and very flat; the trees are very green and there is much water. In the centre of it, there is a very large lake; there is no mountain, and all is so green that it is a pleasure to gaze upon it. The people also are very gentle and, since they long to possess something of ours and fear that nothing will be given to them unless they give something, when they have nothing, they take what they can and immediately throw themselves into the water and swim. But all that they do possess, they give for anything which is given to them, so that they exchange things even for pieces of broken dishes and bits of broken glass cups. . . ."

from Cecil Jane, trans., *The Journal of Christopher Columbus* (New York: Bonanza Books, 1989), 23–28.

Discussion Questions

1. What impressed you the most about this excerpt from Columbus's journal?
2. What is Columbus's main interest on the island? Why is he interested in that?
3. What do you think is Columbus's attitude toward the Taino? Point out passages that reveal his thoughts and feelings about them.

PRIMARY SOURCE *from Travels and Works of*
Captain John Smith

Captain John Smith recorded his experiences in colonial Virginia, including this account of his capture by the Powhatan and his rescue by Chief Powhatan's daughter Pocahontas. As you read, keep in mind that Smith refers to himself in the third person and that only the most confusing of his 17th-century English spellings have been changed.

How Powhatan entertained him. At last they brought him [Smith] to *Meronocomoco [5 Jan. 1608]*, where was *Powhatan* their Emperor. Here more than two hundred of those grim Courtiers stood wondering at him, as he had beene a monster; till *Powhatan* and his traine had put themselves in their greatest braveries [finest clothing]. Before a fire upon a seat like a bedsted, he sat covered with a great robe, made of *Rarowcun* [raccoon] skinnes, and all tailes hanging by. On either hand did sit a young wench [woman] of 16 or 18 yeares, and along on each side the house, two rowes of men, and behind them as many women, with all their heads and shoulders painted red: many of their heads bedecked with the white downe of Birds; but every one with something: and a great chaine of white beads about their necks.

How Pocahontas saved his life. At his entrance before the King, all the people gave a great shout. The Queen of *Appamatuck* was appointed to bring him water to wash his hands, and another brought him a bunch of feathers, in stead of a Towell to dry them: having feasted him after their best barbarous manner they could, a long consultation was held, but the conclusion was, two great stones were brought before Powhatan: then as many as could laid hands on him, dragged him to them, and thereon laid his head, and being ready with their clubs, to beate out his braines, *Pocahontas* the Kings dearest daughter, when no intreaty could prevaile, got his head under her arms, and laid her owne upon his to save him from death: whereat the Emperour was contented he should live to make him hatchets, and her bells, beads, and copper; for they thought him aswell [as capable] of all occupations as themselves. For the King himselfe will make his owne robes, shooes, bowes, arrowes, pots; plant, hunt, or doe any thing so well as the rest. . . .

How Powhatan sent him to James Towne. Two dayes after *[7 Jan. 1608]*, *Powhatan* having disguised himselfe in the most fearfullest manner he could, caused Captain *Smith* to be brought forth to a great house in the woods, and there upon a mat by the fire to be left alone. Not long after from behinde a mat that divided the house, was made the most dolefullest noise he ever heard; then *Powhatan* more like a devill then a man, with some two hundred more as blacke as himselfe, came unto him and told him now they were friends, and presently he should goe to *James* towne, to send him two great gunnes, and a grindstone, for which he would give him the Country of *Capahowosick*, and for ever esteeme him as his sonne *Nantaquoud*.

So to *James* towne with 12 guides Powhatan sent him. That night [7 Jan. 1608] they quarterd in the woods, he still expecting (as he had done all this long time of his imprisonment) every houre to be put to one death or other: for all their feasting. But almightie God (by his divine providence) had mollified the hearts of those sterne *Barbarians* with compassion. The next morning *[8 Jan.]* betimes they came to the Fort.

from Edward Arber, ed., re-edited with an introduction by A. G. Bradley, *Travels and Works of Captain John Smith, 1580–1631* (Edinburgh, Scotland: 1910).

Discussion Questions

1. How was Smith treated by the Powhatan people?
2. According to Smith, why did Chief Powhatan decide to spare Smith's life?
3. Why do you think that the English and the Powhatan people had such an uneasy relationship? Cite possible reasons based on Smith's account and on your textbook.

REVIEW CHAPTER 1

Section 4

PRIMARY SOURCE *from* **The Autobiography**
by Benjamin Franklin

In this excerpt from his autobiography, Franklin reveals the curiosity and excitement about science that was characteristic of the Enlightenment.

In 1746 being at Boston, I met there with a Dr Spence, who was lately arrived from Scotland, and show'd me some electric Experiments. They were imperfectly perform'd, as he was not very expert; but being on a Subject quite new to me, they equally surpriz'd and pleas'd me. Soon after my Return to Philadelphia, our Library Company receiv'd from Mr Peter Colinson, F.R.S. of London a Present of a Glass Tube, with some Account of the Use of it in making such Experiments. I eagerly seiz'd the Opportunity of repeating what I had seen at Boston, and by much Practice acquir'd great Readiness in performing those also which we had an Account of from England, adding a Number of new Ones.—I say much Practice, for my House was continually full for some time, with People who came to see these new Wonders. To divide a little this Incumbrance among my Friends, I caused a Number of similar Tubes to be blown at our Glass-House, with which they furnish'd themselves, so that we had at length several Performers. Among these the principal was Mr Kinnersley, an ingenious Neighbour, who being out of Business, I encouraged to undertake showing the Experiments for Money, and drew up for him two Lectures, in which the Experiments were rang'd in such Order and accompanied with Explanations, in such Method, as that the foregoing should assist in Comprehending the following. He procur'd an elegant Apparatus for the purpose, in which all the little Machines that I had roughly made for myself, were nicely form'd by Instrument-makers. His Lectures were well attended and gave great Satisfaction; and after some time he went thro' the Colonies exhibiting them in every capital Town, and pick'd up some Money. In the West India Islands indeed it was with Difficulty the Experim. could be made, from the general Moisture of the Air.

Oblig'd as we were to Mr Colinson for his Present of the Tube, &c. I thought it right he should be inform'd of our Success in using it, and wrote him several Letters containing Accounts of our Experiments. He got them read in the Royal Society, where they were not at first thought worth so much Notice as to be printed in their Transactions. One Paper which I wrote for Mr. Kinnersley, on the Sameness of Lightning with Electricity, I sent to Dr. Mitchel, an Acquaintance of mine, and one of the Members also of that Society; who wrote me word that it had been read but was laught at by the Connoisseurs: The Papers however being shown to Dr Fothergill, he thought them of too much value to be stifled, and advis'd the Printing of them [in a book]. . . .

What gave my Book . . . sudden and general Celebrity [in Europe], was the Success of one of its propos'd Experiments, made by Messrs Dalibard & Delor, at Marly; for drawing Lightning from the Clouds. This engag'd the public Attention every where. M. Delor, who had an Apparatus for experimental Philosophy, and lectur'd in that Branch of Science, undertook to repeat what he call'd the *Philadelphia Experiments,* and after they were performed before the King & Court, all the Curious of Paris flock'd to see them. I will not swell this Narrative with an Account of that capital Experiment, nor of the infinite Pleasure I receiv'd in the Success of a similar one I made soon after with a Kite at Philadelphia, as both are to be found in the Histories of Electricity.

from Benjamin Franklin, *Writings* (New York: The Library of America, 1987), 1452–1455.

Research Options

1. Research one of Benjamin Franklin's scientific discoveries or inventions. Then give an oral report on what effects that invention has had on our world today.
2. Find out more about the Enlightenment. Then write a paragraph in which you explain how this excerpt from Franklin's autobiography reflects the influence of this movement.

REVIEW CHAPTER

1

Section 2

LITERATURE SELECTION *from* **The Memoirs of Christopher Columbus: A Novel**

by Stephen Marlowe

The Memoirs of Christopher Columbus *is a fictionalized account of the life of the legendary explorer. This excerpt depicts the historic first encounter of Columbus and his crew with the Taino in 1492. As you read, imagine how you would have reacted if you had been a Taino or a crew member.*

We pull steadily for the shore, ten men in each caravel's boat, a round dozen in *Santa Maria's.* For once even the slovenly Pinzón brothers, who have trimmed their beards and slicked down their hair over their close-set eyes, look presentable. They have broken out new clothes that can almost pass for uniforms—clean white jerkins, black velvet doublets, black tights. Oarsmen, musketeers and crossbowmen wear clean, sun-bleached jerkins and hose. As we approach the shore I stand in the prow to unfurl the colors of Castile and León, the golden castle and the purple lion, and the red and yellow stripes of Aragon.

Behind us *Santa Maria, Niña* and *Pinta* ride at anchor in a bay sheltered by reefs of a porous pink coral the likes of which no European has ever seen. Ahead is a dazzling crescent of white sand beach, and beyond the beach a wall of green jungle. The surf here on the western side of the island (where we have sailed, seeking a safe passage through the reefs) is gentle.

As we sweep close to that dazzling beach, I experience an intense yet dreamlike feeling that I have stood in this boat's prow before, and yet, paradoxically, that this is the first day of Creation.

"Up oars!" shouts Peralonso Niño and in unison eighteen oars flash skyward. A wind ruffles the royal standard; I can feel it tug at the staff. A single large green and yellow bird darts close and raucously welcomes us with a voice eerily human. The three boats simultaneously scrape bottom. I raise one bare foot over the gunwale.

But wait—this is a historic moment.

As I take that first step ashore, do I say something deathless and profoundly appropriate, casting my words like a challenge down the corridors of history to intrepid explorers as yet unborn?

Am I prepared for it? As I take that first step ashore, do I say something deathless and profoundly appropriate, casting my words like a challenge down the corridors of history to intrepid explorers as yet unborn? Do I perhaps say, as I plant the royal banner on the beach, "One small step for a Christian, one giant step for Christendom," thus beating Neil Armstrong by almost 500 years?

No, there are no half-billion T.V. viewers around the world to watch me, no periodical has purchased the serial rights to my adventures for a king's ransom, no publisher has advanced an even greater fortune for *Columbus's Journal* (so-called), no mission control exists to monitor my every move. Only the citizens of Palos, and a few score people at that Peripatetic Royal Court visiting God-knows-where in Spain right now, even suspect we have crossed the vastness of the Ocean Sea to this small and lovely tropical island, part of the Indian archipelago, I am convinced, with fabled gold-roofed Cipango just over the horizon.

So I do not utter wisdom for the ages.

What do I say, uneasily and with reason, as I nudge Peralonso Niño, is: "There's someone in the woods over there."

We all freeze, our eyes scanning the foliage (sun-dappled, secret, alien). Again there is a flash of movement, and suddenly there they are, no longer in the woods but coming out.

"Crossbowmen, front!" says Martín Alonzo, but I raise a hand and shake my head.

These natives of the Indian archipelago are but ten in number and not only unarmed, except for small harmless-looking spears with fish-tooth points, but naked. They are neither black-skinned (as might have been expected, according to Aristotle, since we are more or less on the same latitude as the west coast of Africa) nor white like Europeans. No, they are an indeterminate shade between, a sort of bronzy color that, with imagination and in dim light, you could almost call red. Tan then, a sort of ruddy tan. Tall, well proportioned, their coarse (but not African kinky) hair worn horse-tail long, their limbs straight and smooth-muscled. They peer at our tall-masted ships at anchor, our boats at the water's edge, ourselves taking our first steps across the dazzling (and hot underfoot) sand—their whole world, their whole conception of the nature of things altered at a stroke forever. And innocently and with a naive delight, they smile.

Inspired, I drop to my knees and thank God for sending us here safely, across that vastness of Ocean Sea, and on both sides of me the men are kneeling, and then I rise and draw my ceremonial sword, jewel-encrusted hilt catching the sunlight, and in fine theatrical style raise it skyward as I plant the royal standard and claim this island for the Kingdoms of Castile, León and Aragon, for Queen Isabel and King Fernando, for Spain, for Christianity. In thanksgiving I name it the Island of the Holy Saviour.

The Indians—for what else can I call natives of this Indies archipelago—come closer to watch the arcane ceremony.

Some crewmen remain on their knees, praying. But Vincente Yáñez Pinzón, neither rising nor praying still, does an odd sort of pivot on his knees to face me and in a humble voice speaks. I won't reproduce the precise, embarrassing words, but on behalf of the men of Niña he apologizes for not giving the Admiral of the Ocean Sea, not to mention the Viceroy of the Indies which I now am, his full trust.

One by one the landing party comes to me to ask forgiveness. Only Juan Cosa and Chachu stand silently by, watching.

"Command us, Viceroy!" passionately exclaims Constable Harana, even as he casts suspicious glances at the advancing Indians who, by this time, have ringed us close so that Martín Alonzo again

The boldest of the bronzy-skinned men approaches me and with a smile and . . . touches my left sleeve, gently rolling the soft velvet between his fingers. It is clear he has never seen a man clothed before.

turns to his crossbowmen and again I must signal him, no.

The boldest of the bronzy-skinned men approaches me and with a smile and a mouthing of gibberish (which anthropologists will later learn is the Arawak language) touches my left sleeve, gently rolling the soft velvet between his fingers. It is clear he has never seen a man clothed before.

I call Luís Torres the interpreter forward.

"Ask him the name of this place, and of himself," I say.

Torres does so, with a show of confidence, in Latin.

The Indian responds incomprehensibly, if musically.

Torres, less confidently, tries Hebrew.

The Indian responds with equal incomprehensibility.

Torres, clearly worried, tries Ladino, Aramaic, Spanish.

Same lack of success.

We all wait for Arabic, that mother of languages.

Torres takes a deep breath and tries Arabic.

And the Indian, who I now realize is a boy of no more than fourteen, throws back his head and laughs.

We all assume this signifies comprehension. But his response is again incomprehensible, if musical.

Gentle, green-eyed, girlishly slim Luís Torres is now desperate. He has come with us, he must feel, under false pretenses.

He tries a sort of sign language, poking his chest and saying, "Torres."

The Indian, grinning, pokes his own chest. "Torres."

Luís Torres sighs and tries again. He spreads his arms broadly to include the beach, the jungle. He bends and scoops up a handful of sand, lets it trickle through his fingers, then spreads his arms again as his expressive face asks a silent question.

The Indian jumps with excitement. "Guanahaní!" he cries. Then he pokes his own chest and makes the same sound: "Guanahaní."

Comprehension comes to Luís Torres. "Their name for this island is Guanahaní and the people call themselves that too—Guanahaní. Get it?"

I get it. Torres and the Guanahaní spokesman continue to smile at each other in a kind of basic sub-linguistic communion.

"Ask him which way's Cipango," says Martín Alonzo, "ask him where's the gold."

But, "One thing at a time," I tell him with a viceregal smile, and send two oarsmen back to Santa Maria's boat for the sea chest full of trinkets, the sort that have proven so popular with the Fan people of West Africa. The chest is set on the sand and with a flourish Pedro Terreros opens it.

"Don't," cautions Rodrigo de Segovia, "give all your trinkets to the very first natives you encounter. Trinkets don't grow on trees."

The royal comptroller fails to curb Pedro's munificence. Out of the sea chest, like a magician, he plucks red wool caps, brass rings, strings of bright glass beads and little round falconry bells.

Collective oohs and ahs come from the Guanahaní as Pedro distributes the trinkets. The bells are the clear favorite. Soon their tinkling fills the air, along with Indian laughter, very like our own.

I send to the boat again, this time for empty oak water casks. Luís Torres goes through a frenzy of sign language to indicate thirst and drinking. The Guanahaní spokesman claps his hands, grins, jumps up and down and jabbers to his cohorts, who lift the casks to their shoulders.

So laden, the Indians (or archipelagans, if you prefer) march off. Constable Harana gives them a suspicious look and I know that Martín Alonzo will call for his crossbowmen again.

"We'll go with them," I say to forestall him, and detail a guard to stay with the boats.

With us lumbering behind, the ten archipelagans slip silently with our casks through the deep shadows of the jungle (bird calls, strange small unidentifiable crunching sounds, cheeps and chirps and pips and squeaks, sudden slithery rushes, frail querulous cries, clicks and howls and mini-grunts, all slightly unnerving) to a spring, where we are not permitted to lift a finger. The Indians draw water, letting us sample its sweetness from a calabash; then we Spaniards sit against the broad reddish-brown

Collective oohs and ahs come from the Guanahaní as Pedro distributes the trinkets. The bells are the clear favorite. Soon their tinkling fills the air, along with Indian laughter, very like our own.

trunks of unfamiliar trees, relaxing as the complexity of jungle noises assumes its proper place as natural background music, and watch the Indians, in high good spirits, *do our work for us. . . .*

"Where's the gold? Ask him, will you? Where's the gold?" Martín Alonzo demands impatiently of Luís Torres as we return to the boats, the archipelagans sagging under the weight of our full water casks.

Second time around, my viceregal smile's a bit forced. "All in good time," I tell Pinzón, not wild about the look on his face—an apparent compression of the small features, a meanness especially around the eyes. Gold fever if ever I saw it. . . .

Who can really blame Martín Alonzo? He knows as well as I that whatever else we find, gold is crucial to the Great Venture. Gold—gold in quantity—will alone persuade the royals to send out a second, larger expedition.

With me in command, naturally. I'm Admiral of the Ocean Sea, not to mention viceroy and governor for life.

Sometimes I dream of myself living the viceregal life in a vast, princely palace in a vast, princely realm. It could happen. In Cathay and Cipango, there's gold aplenty. Marco Polo said so, and he was there.

But where, exactly, are *we?*

Activity Options

1. With a small group of classmates, write a skit about Columbus's first encounter with the Tainos in 1492. To get a better sense of Columbus's character, also refer to the excerpt from Columbus's journal (on pages 26–27). Then assign roles and perform your skit for the class.

2. Jot down vivid descriptive details, such as what two crewmen wore (white jerkins, black velvet doublets, black tights), that you find in this excerpt. Then draw a sketch to illustrate the first encounter.

REVIEW CHAPTER

1

Section 3

AMERICAN LIVES John Winthrop
Man of Principle, Man of God

"We shall be as a City upon a Hill, the eyes of all people are upon us, so that if we shall deal falsely with our God . . . we shall open the mouths of enemies to speak evil of the ways of God."—John Winthrop, "A Model of Christian Charity" (1630)

Well-educated, John Winthrop (1588–1649) was also a Puritan who believed that the English church needed reforming. He set aside his country estate in England and agreed to join a new venture: planting a colony in North America. As one of the leaders of that new colony, he helped shape how Americans see themselves.

Winthrop trained as an attorney and enjoyed a successful law career for many years, living comfortably in a country manor. He suffered tragedy as well, losing two wives. His third marriage, though, lasted thirty years, however, and that wife joined him later in Massachusetts.

In 1629, he began to listen to those talking of a colony in North America. Many friends advised against the idea, but Winthrop carefully listed the pluses and minuses—and decided to join. Winthrop was willing to leave England because economic troubles had cut his income and political problems cost him his position as attorney. Like the other Puritan leaders, he was also convinced that the best hope for reforming the church was to take it away from England. He quickly became influential among the leaders, who chose Winthrop as governor shortly before the Massachusetts Bay Company sailed to North America in 1630. Determined to control the fate of the colony, the leaders took the company charter with them. As a result, they were relatively free of interference from the British government.

As hundreds of colonists sailed for their new home, Winthrop wrote "A Model of Christian Charity," setting forth the principles underlying the colony. He said that the colony's goal was "to improve our lives to do more service to the Lord." He emphasized that the colonists joined "by mutual consent" to seek a home—the "city upon a hill"—under a "government both civil and ecclesiastical." He closed by urging the colonists to work together "that we and our seed may live by obeying His voice and cleaving to Him."

Winthrop dominated Massachusetts in its early years, serving as governor or deputy governor for most of the colony's first two decades. He and other leaders—many from the clergy—served as magistrates and set policy for the colony. Some of their decisions have had lasting effect. They set aside one area of Boston—the Common—as public property for common use, which it remains to this day. They created the Boston Latin School and Harvard University and told the various towns in the colony to start schools, launching American public education. Ironically, students schooled in these institutions later challenged the colony's conservative leaders.

Winthrop did not believe in democracy. He felt that leaders knew what was best for the people. He wrote that the magistrates must have the power of vetoing the actions of the people. Democracy was wrong, he said, because "there was no such government in Israel."

However, Winthrop was always strictly honest. When voted out of office the first time, his successor ordered that the colony's accounts be examined, a veiled slap at Winthrop's conduct. The audit showed that everything was in perfect order—in fact, Winthrop had loaned the colony some of his own funds to meet expenses. His agent in England was less fair to him, however, and Winthrop lost money due to his dishonesty. For the remainder of his life, Winthrop was financially strapped. However, he was often elected to one-year terms as governor, and his son John Winthrop, Jr., (1606–1676) became a respected colonial governor of Connecticut.

Questions

1. What did Winthrop mean by calling the colony a "city upon a hill"?
2. Why did Winthrop leave his advantages in England for uncertainty in Massachusetts?
3. On what basis did Winthrop reject democracy, and what does this show about his political beliefs?

AMERICAN LIVES Olaudah Equiano
Freed Slave, Early Abolitionist

"I now offer this edition of my Narrative . . . hoping it may still be the means . . . [of] strengthening the [movement] . . . to put a speedy end to a traffic both cruel and unjust."—*Olaudah Equiano,* The Interesting Narrative of the Life of Olaudah Equiano *(1792 edition)*

Olaudah Equiano, captured in Africa and sold into slavery, survived the deadly middle passage. He eventually bought his freedom and later wrote his autobiography, considered by writer Arna Bontemps as "the first truly notable book in the genre now known as slave narratives."

Equiano was born in present-day Nigeria around 1745. He remembered much of his childhood and noted the customs and traditions of his village. He called the "manner of living" in his remote village "entirely plain," describing his people's hard work, modest manners, and lack of alcoholic beverages.

At age ten, Equiano and his sister were kidnapped by slavers. Placed on a ship bound for the Americas, he saw the horror of the middle passage. White sailors' cruelty surprised him, as he had never seen such actions—and he was surprised even more when a sailor was flogged, for it shocked him that they would be cruel to each other. "This made me fear these people the more," he remembered. After describing how two Africans jumped overboard rather than continue the voyage, he reminded his readers of how the middle passage violated Christian morality: "O, ye nominal Christians! might not an African ask you, learned you this from your God . . . ?"

Equiano was sold to a Virginia planter, on whose land he stayed for a brief time. Then a British naval officer, Michael Henry Pascal, bought him. The officer renamed him Gustavus Vassa after a Swedish noble who helped liberate Sweden from the Dutch. Equiano used the name for the remainder of his life in western society—but he put his real name on the title page of his autobiography.

Equiano served aboard ship with Pascal for many years, seeing action against the French in Canada and the Mediterranean. He learned to read and write and was baptized. Though Pascal had promised him freedom, he was sold again in 1762. Equiano felt betrayed, his "heart ready to burst with sorrow and anguish."

For three years, Equiano worked for a ship captain who traded between the West Indies and British North America. In 1766, he used money he had saved to buy his freedom. "My feet scarcely touched the ground," he recalled, "for they were winged with joy." In his book, he recalled that he thought of the words of a Psalm: "I glorified God in my heart, in whom I trusted."

Equiano became a skilled seaman. He captained one ship when the captain died and on another voyage saved the crew when the ship became wrecked. Rescued from this mishap, he ended up in Georgia, where he escaped being kidnapped and probably sold into slavery again.

Later Equiano joined a sea voyage seeking a Northeast Passage from Europe to Asia and tried to establish a plantation in Central America. He settled in England and married in 1792. Various accounts put his death between 1797 and 1801.

Equiano's autobiography was first published in 1789 and was immediately popular. It ended with a long argument for abolishing the "inhuman traffic" of the slave trade. Like others of his time, Equiano hoped that this would be the first step toward abolishing slavery. In addition to making moral arguments against the slave trade, he offered economic reasons. He hoped to convince British leaders that their trade would grow if carried on with an Africa freed of the specter of slavery.

Questions

1. What point was Equiano trying to make by including details about life in Africa?
2. What was Equiano's purpose in describing the cruel treatment he witnessed on the middle passage?
3. Why do you think Equiano used both moral and economic arguments to urge ending the slave trade?

Name _____ Date _____

GUIDED READING *Colonial Resistance and Rebellion*

A. As you read this section, fill in the chart to trace the following sequence of events.

1a. The British Parliament passed the Stamp Act (1765) in order to . . .	**b.** Colonists responded to the act by . . .	**c.** Britain responded to the colonists by . . .
2a. The British Parliament passed the Townshend Act (1767) in order to . . .	**b.** Colonists responded to the act by . . .	**c.** Britain responded to the colonists by . . .
3a. The British Parliament passed the Tea Act (1773) in order to . . .	**b.** Colonists responded to the act by . . .	**c.** Britain responded to the colonists by . . .
4a. The British Parliament passed the Intolerable Acts (1774) in order to . . .	**b.** Colonists responded to the act by . . .	**c.** Britain responded to the colonists by . . .

B. On the back of this paper, identify or explain each of the following:

committees of correspondence **Battle of Bunker Hill** **Thomas Jefferson**
Second Continental Congress *Common Sense* **Declaration of Independence**

Name _____ Date _____

GUIDED READING *The War for Independence*

Section 2

A. As you read this section, write answers to the questions about each of the
Revolutionary War battles listed below.

	Who won?	Why did they win?	What were the important results?
1. New York			
2. Trenton			
3. Saratoga			
4. Yorktown			

B. Summarize the difficulties faced by each group of Patriots during the Revolutionary War.

Patriots	What were some of the hardships they faced?
1. Soldiers	
2. Members of Congress	
3. Civilians	

C. On the back of this paper, identify or define each of the following:

Loyalists   **Patriots**   **Marquis de Lafayette**   **Treaty of Paris**   **egalitarianism**

Name _____ Date _____

A. As you read about how the Constitution was developed, complete the chart below
to summarize the issues that arose.

1. The Virginia Plan proposed a Congress composed of:	2. The New Jersey Plan called for a Congress consisting of:

↓

3. The Virginia Plan proposed that representation in Congress be based on: Other large states agreed.	4. The New Jersey Plan proposed that congressional representation be based on: Other small states agreed.
5. How did the Great Compromise resolve this conflict?	

↓

6. Northern states felt that representation in Congress should be based on the number of:	7. Southern states felt that representation should be based on the number of:
8. How did the Three-Fifths Compromise resolve this conflict?	

B. On the back of this paper, use the terms *Federalists*, *Antifederalists*, *Bill of Rights*,
and *ratification* in a paragraph.

Name _____   Date _____

REVIEW
CHAPTER

2

Section 4

GUIDED READING *Launching the New Nation*

A. Fill out the chart below, taking notes about Washington's two terms as president.

Government Organization	
1. What did the Judiciary Act of 1789 establish?	2. What departments did Washington create and whom did he appoint to head them?

Philosophies of Government	
3. How did Jefferson feel about political power and the common people?	4. How did Hamilton feel about political power and the common people?
5. Why did Jefferson and Madison oppose the national bank?	6. Why did Hamilton support the national bank?

Party Politics	
7. To which party did Jefferson belong?	8. To which party did Hamilton belong?
9. Which region in general supported the Federalists? The Democratic-Republicans?	

B. On the back of this paper, identify or explain each of the following:

Thomas Pinckney   **Battle of Fallen Timbers**   **John Jay**   **Alien and Sedition Acts**

Name _____ Date _____

REVIEW CHAPTER
2
Section

BUILDING VOCABULARY *Revolution and the Early Republic*

A. Multiple Choice Circle the letter before the term or name that best completes the sentence.

1. The first tax measure to affect the colonists directly by imposing levies on many everyday items was known as the (a) Sugar Act (b) Stamp Act (c) Intolerable Acts (d) Quartering Act.

2. A key Enlightenment thinker whose idea of social contract between people and their government appealed to colonial leaders was (a) Thomas Paine (b) Samuel Adams (c) John Locke (d) Marquis de Lafayette.

3. Those colonists who opposed independence and remained loyal to the British king were known as (a) Loyalists (b) Patriots (c) minutemen (d) Hessians.

4. Under the Articles of Confederation, the federal government could not (a) declare war (b) borrow money (c) establish a postal service (d) impose taxes

5. Critics of the Sedition Act argued that it violated (a) freedom of speech (b) freedom of religion (c) the right to bear arms (d) the right to privacy.

B. Matching Match the definition in the second column with the word in the first column. Write the appropriate letter next to the word.

_____ 1. nullification   a. pamphlet calling on colonists to support independence

_____ 2. cabinet   b. bribery scandal involving United States and France

_____ 3. Thomas Jefferson   c. turning point battle of the Revolutionary War

_____ 4. Yorktown   d. principle that states had the right to void acts of Congress

_____ 5. republic   e. first ten amendments of the Constitution

_____ 6. Bill of Rights   f. principle author of the Declaration of Independence

_____ 7. XYZ Affair   g. rule by citizens through elected

_____ 8. Common Sense   h. president's chief advisers

_____ 9. Saratoga   i. system to keep one branch of government from becoming too powerful

_____ 10. checks and balances   j. site of British surrender

C. Writing Imagine you are a political reporter during the early years of the republic. Write a brief news article about the debate over the U.S. Constitution using the following words correctly.

Checks and balances   **ratification**   **Federalist**

Antifederalists   **Bill of Rights**

SKILLBUILDER PRACTICE *Analyzing Causes and Effects*

REVIEW CHAPTER

2

Section 2

Without help from France, the course of the Revolutionary War might have gone quite differently for American forces. To learn more about the causes and effects of French involvement, read the passage below. Then, as you complete the cause-and-effect diagram at the bottom of the page, notice how effects can turn into causes. (See Skillbuilder Handbook, p. R7.)

French and British Conflicts in North America Long before the American Revolutionary War, France and Britain had been enemies. Disputes over ownership of North American territories and the rights to fur trading and fishing there led to the French and Indian War. Although the French were successful at first, the British eventually defeated them. As a result, France lost most of its North American territory to Britain.

After suffering these losses, France was anxious to challenge Britain again and regain her colonies. For this reason King Louis XVI of France considered joining the American side against the British in the Revolutionary War in North America.

Before he would commit French soldiers and ships to the war, however, Louis XVI wanted proof that

American troops could win a major battle on their own. The American victory he had been looking for came in October 1777, when British troops surrendered to American forces after the Battle of Saratoga.

The French and American Alliance Four months after the Battle of Saratoga, France formally recognized the United States as an independent country. In June 1778, France declared war with Britain. French soldiers began arriving in the summer of 1780 to fight alongside Patriot forces, and within a year, they were contributing to U.S. victories. In September 1781, French ships forced a British naval fleet to leave Chesapeake Bay, setting the stage for the defeat of the British by the combined U.S. and French forces at Yorktown, the last significant battle of the war.

1. CAUSE: France loses North American colonies to Britain during the French and Indian War.

2. EFFECT/CAUSE:

3. CAUSE: In a major American victory during the Revolutionary War, Americans defeat the British at the Battle of Saratoga in 1777.

4. EFFECT/CAUSE: France recognizes the United States and declares war against Britain.

5. EFFECT/CAUSE:

7. EFFECT/CAUSE: French ships force the British out of Chesapeake Bay.

6. EFFECT: French and American soldiers are victorious against British troops.

8. EFFECT:

Name _____ Date _____

REVIEW CHAPTER

2

Section 3

SKILLBUILDER PRACTICE *Interpreting Charts*

As the battle between the colonists and British began, each side had its strengths and weaknesses. Examine the chart shown here showing what each side brought to the battle and then answer the questions below. (See Skillbuilder Handbook, p. R30.)

1. Which side had the stronger, better-equipped military?

_____

_____

2. Why would a large distance separating Britain and the battlefields be a problem for the British?

_____

_____

3. How might familiarity of the home ground help the colonists' war effort?

_____

_____

4. Which side would you have predicted to win the war based on the chart? Why?

_____

_____

Military Strengths and Weaknesses	
UNITED STATES	**GREAT BRITAIN**

Strengths	Weaknesses	Strengths	Weaknesses
· familiarity of home ground · leadership of George Washington and other officers · inspiring cause—independence	· most soldiers untrained and undisciplined · shortage of food and ammunition · inferior navy · no central government to enforce wartime policies	· strong, well-trained army and navy · strong central government with available funds · support of colonial Loyalists and Native Americans	· large distance separating Britain from battlefields · troops unfamiliar with terrain · weak military leaders · sympathy of certain British politicans for the American cause

Name _____ Date _____

SKILLBUILDER PRACTICE *Comparing; Contrasting*

Although Thomas Jefferson and Alexander Hamilton both made significant contributions to shaping the future of the United States, they were total opposites in many ways. After reading the passage below, fill out the chart. First, list five categories that you'd like to use in contrasting them. Two have been listed for you. Then, list differences between the two men for the categories. (See Skillbuilder Handbook, p. R8.)

Thomas Jefferson Known as the author of the Declaration of Independence and third president of the United States, Thomas Jefferson was also a noted diplomat and thinker. He was born on his family's farm and led the life of a country boy.

When Jefferson was 14 years old, his father died, and the boy inherited the family farm. At the age of 16 he began attending the College of William and Mary in Williamsburg, Virginia. After college he studied law and began to practice law in 1767. He served in Virginia government and was chosen as a delegate to the Second Continental Congress. In 1776 he drafted the Declaration of Independence.

Instead of fighting in the Revolutionary War, Jefferson worked for social reform in Virginia. Following the war, he resumed his participation in the national government, eventually becoming president, with Aaron Burr as his vice-president.

After two terms as president, Jefferson retired from political life. He died quietly at his home on July 4, 1826.

Alexander Hamilton Born in the West Indies, Alexander Hamilton was the son of a Scottish merchant there. He spent some of his youth working for a trading company on the island of St. Croix, then traveled to North America and attended King's College, which later became Columbia University. He served as a captain during the Revolutionary War.

In 1782, Alexander Hamilton began to practice law in New York and became a delegate to the Congress of the Confederation under the Articles of Confederation. He was appointed secretary of the treasury in 1789. In 1795, after increased Congressional opposition to his ideas, Hamilton resigned as treasury secretary, but he remained active in politics.

In the presidential election of 1800, Hamilton supported Thomas Jefferson because, although he distrusted Jefferson, he disliked Jefferson's opponent, Aaron Burr, even more. Jefferson won the election and Burr became vice-president. In 1804, Hamilton's public criticism of Burr resulted in a duel between the two men. On July 11, 1804, they fought. Hamilton was shot and died from his wound the next day.

Category	Jefferson	Hamilton
1. Place of birth		
2. Youth		
3.		
4.		
5.		

Name _____ Date _____

REVIEW CHAPTER 2 Section 1

RETEACHING ACTIVITY *Colonial Resistance and Rebellion*

Finding Main Ideas

The following questions deal with events that led up to the American Revolution. Answer them in the space provided.

1. Why did the Stamp Act so anger the colonists?

_____

_____

2. What event prompted passage of the Intolerable Acts? What did the acts do?

_____

_____

3. When did the Second Continental Congress meet? What actions did it take?

_____

_____

4. What was the reaction of King George to the Olive Branch petition?

_____

_____

5. For what reasons did the writer Thomas Paine urge colonists to support independence?

_____

_____

6. How did colonial leaders justify their declaration of independence from Britain?

_____

_____

Name _____   Date _____

REVIEW CHAPTER
2
Section 2

RETEACHING ACTIVITY *The War for Independence*

A. Sequencing

Number the events of the Revolutionary War below in the order in which they occurred.

_____ 1. France signs an alliance with the Americans.

_____ 2. Charles Cornwallis captures Charles Town, South Carolina.

_____ 3. The Continental Army retreats from New York.

_____ 4. Two sides sign the Treaty of Paris.

_____ 5. Americans defeat British at Battle of Saratoga.

_____ 6. British troops capture Philadelphia.

_____ 7. Washington leads troops across Delaware River and captures Trenton.

_____ 8. British surrender at Yorktown.

B. Evaluating

Write *T* in the blank if the statement is true. If the statement is false, write *F* in the blank and then write the corrected statement on the line below.

_____ 1. Those colonists who supported independence were know as Loyalists.

_____

_____ 2. The American victory at Saratoga was important because it prompted France to enter the side of the colonists.

_____

_____ 3. The Continental Army spent the winter of 1777–1778 in comfortable conditions in Philadelphia.

_____

_____ 4. About 5,000 African Americans fought for the colonial cause in the Continental Army.

_____

_____ 5. The American Revolution brought equal rights to all Americans.

_____

Name _____ Date _____

REVIEW
CHAPTER
2
Section 3

RETEACHING ACTIVITY *Confederation and the Constitution*

Analyzing

Complete the chart below by describing the various conflicts and compromises involved in creating and ratifying the U.S. Constitution.

	Conflict	Compromise
Large state v. Small state		
North v. South		
Ratification		

REVIEW CHAPTER 2

Section 4

RETEACHING ACTIVITY *Launching the New Nation*

Reading Comprehension

Choose the best answer for each item. Write the letter of your answer in the blank.

_____ 1. The nation's first Secretary of State was
  a. Alexander Hamilton.
  b. Thomas Jefferson.
  c. James Madison.
  d. John Jay

_____ 2. Those who supported a strong central government were known as
  a. Whigs.
  b. Democratic-Republicans.
  c. Federalists.
  d. Antifederalists.

_____ 3. Alexander Hamilton's economic plan called for the federal government to
  a. pay off its debts.
  b. increase spending.
  c. collect more taxes from the states.
  d. borrow money from other nations.

_____ 4. In his farewell address, George Washington warned the nation to avoid
  a. neutrality in foreign affairs.
  b. conflicts with Native Americans.
  c. westward expansion.
  d. alliances with other nations.

_____ 5. The XYZ Affair brought the United States to the brink of war with
  a. France.
  b. Spain.
  c. Great Britain.
  d. the Netherlands.

_____ 6. The Virginia and Kentucky resolutions asserted the principle of
  a. judicial review.
  b. nullification.
  c. majority rule.
  d. egalitarianism.

Name _____ Date _____

REVIEW
CHAPTER
2
Section 2

GEOGRAPHY APPLICATION: PLACE *The Siege of Yorktown*

Directions: Read the paragraphs below and study the maps carefully. Then answer the questions that follow.

In the late spring of 1781, the British general Cornwallis marched his troops northward out of North Carolina and in July set up camp at Yorktown, Virginia. Yorktown is on a peninsula at the point where the York River meets Chesapeake Bay. While fighting to take all of Virginia, Cornwallis wanted to be connected with other British troops in New York by sea and with the British naval forces in the Atlantic.

However, a French fleet of 24 ships in Chesapeake Bay was able to seal off the waters to the east. Meanwhile, Generals Washington and Rochambeau led American and French troops south-

ward toward Yorktown and joined up with Lafayette. They surrounded Yorktown and began hitting the town with cannon fire. This final battle of the Revolutionary War was fought just a few miles from Jamestown, the site of the first permanent English settlement on the continent.

The map below shows the positions of the British and of the Americans and their French allies at Yorktown. On October 17, American and French cannon fire increased on Yorktown, which was then low on ammunition. On the 19th, the British troops surrendered.

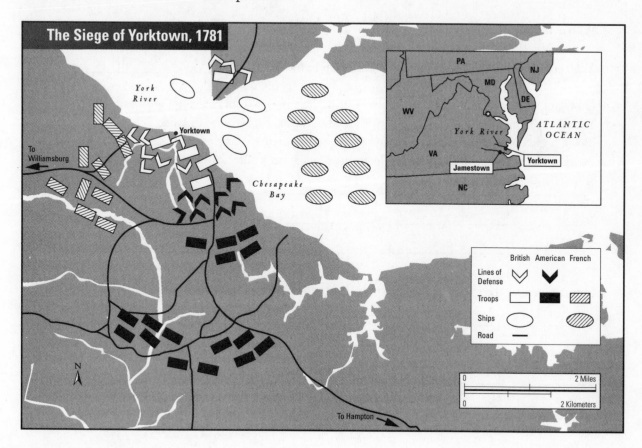

Interpreting Text and Visuals

1. Why was Yorktown seemingly a good place for Cornwallis to establish
   fortifications? _____

   _____

   _____

2. Why was Cornwallis unable to be reinforced by British ships entering
   Chesapeake Bay? _____

   _____

   Why could he not be reinforced by British ships coming down the York River
   from the west? _____

   _____

3. Who controlled the roads leading from Yorktown to the south? _____

   Who controlled the roads leading from Yorktown to the west? _____

4. On October 16, a violent storm prevented Cornwallis's troops from crossing the
   York River at night to a peninsula of British land to the north. Most boats were
   blown back a mile or more below Yorktown. Based on the map, how might the
   weather have influenced Cornwallis's decision to finally surrender within days?

   _____

   _____

   _____

5. Summarize how the geography of Yorktown led to the defeat of the British.

   _____

   _____

   _____

6. What is ironic about the English presence in North America coming to an end
   at Yorktown? _____

   _____

   _____

PRIMARY SOURCE The Boston Tea Party

On the night of December 16, 1773, George Hewes disguised himself as a Mohawk and helped dump 342 chests of tea into Boston Harbor to protest the British Tea Act. As you read Hewes's account of the Boston Tea Party, think about the causes and effects of the rebels' protest.

The tea destroyed was contained in three ships, lying near each other at what was called at that time Griffin's wharf, and were surrounded by armed ships of war. The commanders had publicly declared that if the rebels, as they were pleased to style the Bostonians, should not withdraw their opposition to the landing of the tea before a certain day, the 17th day of December, 1773, they should on that day force it on shore, under the cover of their cannon's mouth. On the day preceding the seventeenth, there was a meeting of the citizens of the county of Suffolk, convened at one of the churches in Boston, for the purpose of consulting on what measures might be considered expedient to prevent the landing of the tea, or secure the people from the collection of the duty. At that meeting a committee was appointed to wait on Governor Hutchinson, and request him to inform them whether he would take any measures to satisfy the people on the object of the meeting.

To the first application of this committee, the Governor told them he would give them a definite answer by five o'clock in the afternoon. At the hour appointed, the committee again repaired to the Governor's house, and on inquiry found he had gone to his country seat at Milton, a distance of about six miles. When the committee returned and informed the meeting of the absence of the Governor, there was a confused murmur among the members, and the meeting was immediately dissolved, many of them crying out, "Let every man do his duty, and be true to his country"; and there was a general huzza for Griffin's wharf.

It was now evening, and I immediately dressed myself in the costume of an Indian, equipped with a small hatchet, which I and my associates denomi-

After having painted my face and hands with coal dust in the shop of a blacksmith, I repaired to Griffin's wharf, where the ships lay that contained the tea.

nated the tomahawk, and a club. After having painted my face and hands with coal dust in the shop of a blacksmith, I repaired to Griffin's wharf, where the ships lay that contained the tea. When I first appeared in the street after being thus disguised, I fell in with many who were dressed, equipped and painted as I was, and who fell in with me and marched in order to the place of our destination.

When we arrived at the wharf, there were three of our number who assumed an authority to direct our operations, to which we readily submitted.

They divided us into three parties, for the purpose of boarding the three ships which contained the tea at the same time. The name of him who commanded the division to which I was assigned was Leonard Pitt. The names of the other commanders I never knew. We were immediately ordered by the respective commanders to board all the ships at the same time, which we promptly obeyed.

The commander of the division to which I belonged, as soon as we were on board the ship, appointed me boatswain, and ordered me to go to the captain and demand of him the keys to the hatches and a dozen candles. I made the demand accordingly, and the captain promptly replied, and delivered the articles; but requested me at the same time to do no damage to the ship or rigging. We then were ordered by our commander to open the hatches and take out all the chests of tea and throw them overboard, and we immediately proceeded to execute his orders, first cutting and splitting the chests with our tomahawks, so as thoroughly to expose them to the effects of the water.

In about three hours from the time we went on board, we had thus broken and thrown overboard every tea chest to be found in the ship, while those in the other ships were disposing of the tea in the same way, at the same time. We were surrounded by British armed ships, but no attempt was made to resist us.

We then quietly retired to our several places of residence, without having any conversation with each other, or taking any measures to discover who were our associates; nor do I recollect of our having had the knowledge of the name of a single individual concerned in that affair, except that of Leonard Pitt, the commander of my division, whom I have mentioned. There appeared to be an understanding that each individual should volunteer his services, keep his own secret, and risk the consequences for himself. No disorder took place during that transaction, and it was observed at that time that the stillest night ensued that Boston had enjoyed for many months.

During the time we were throwing the tea overboard, there were several attempts made by some of the citizens of Boston and its vicinity to carry off small quantities of it for their family use. To effect that object, they would watch their opportunity to snatch up a handful from the deck, where it became plentifully scattered, and put it into their pockets. One Captain O'Connor, whom I well knew, came on board for that purpose, and when he supposed he was not noticed, filled his pockets, and also the lining of his coat. But I had detected him and gave information to the captain of what he was doing. We were ordered to take him into custody, and just as he was stepping from the vessel, I seized him by the skirt of his coat, and in attempting to pull him back, I tore it off; but, springing forward, by a rapid effort he made his escape. He had, however, to run a gauntlet through the crowd upon the wharf, each one, as he passed, giving him a kick or a stroke.

Another attempt was made to save a little tea from the ruins of the cargo by a tall, aged man who wore a large cocked hat and white wig, which was fashionable at that time. He had sleightly [secretly] slipped a little into his pocket, but being detected,

they seized him and, taking his hat and wig from his head, threw them, together with the tea, of which they had emptied his pockets, into the water. In consideration of his advanced age, he was permitted to escape, with now and then a slight kick.

The next morning, after we had cleared the ships of the tea, it was discovered that very considerable quantities of it were floating upon the surface of the water; and to prevent the possibility of any of its being saved for use, a number of small boats were manned by sailors and citizens, who rowed them into those parts of the harbor wherever tea was visible, and by beating it with oars and paddles so thoroughly drenched it as to render its entire destruction inevitable.

from Richard B. Morris and James Woodress, eds., *Voices From America's Past*, vol. 2, *The Colonies and the New Nation* (New York: Dutton, 1963), 77–79.

Activity Options

1. Make a cause-and-effect diagram like this one to illustrate causes and effects of the Boston Tea Party described in this eyewitness account.

2. Work with your classmates to plan a reenactment of the Boston Tea Party. Choose roles, including Hewes, Leonard Pitt, and Captain O'Connor, and then dramatize the events described in Hewes's firsthand account. Also, use details in Hewes's account to help you decide about props, costumes, dialogue, and so forth. Rehearse your dramatization and then present it to your class.

3. The Boston Tea Party was an extreme form of protest against the Tea Act. What other forms of protest might angry Bostonians have used? Design a poster, a button, a protest song, or a slogan that protests the Tea Act and share it with your classmates.

Name _____ Date _____

PRIMARY SOURCE Political Cartoon

After the Declaration of Independence, American colonists were torn between remaining loyal to Britain and seeking independence. Approximately 60,000 Loyalists fled the country; others remained and faced persecution. Study this British political cartoon to find out how Loyalists such as William Franklin feared they would be treated by America (portrayed as an Indian maiden).

SHELB–NS SACRIFICE or the recommended Loyalists, a faithful representation of a Tragedy shortly to be performed on the Continent of America. Invented by Cruelty. Engraved by Dishonour. Line engraving, 1783.

Research Options

1. To the right of center in the cartoon is Lord Shelburne, the British prime minister in 1783. Find out more about him to discover why Britain (portrayed as a British maiden with spear and shield) calls him a hypocrite and a Patriot (portrayed as an Indian) says "Shelbu–n for ever." Report your findings to the class.

2. Did Loyalists meet the bloody fate forecasted in the cartoon? Find out more about what happened to Loyalists before, during, and after the American Revolution. Prepare a chart to illustrate the political, economic, social, and physical challenges that Loyalists faced.

REVIEW CHAPTER 2

Section 2

PRIMARY SOURCE *from* Valley Forge Diary

After he reached the winter quarters where General George Washington camped with his army, the 27-year-old surgeon Albigence Waldo recorded in his diary the desperate conditions that he encountered at Valley Forge, Pennsylvania. As you read this portion of Waldo's diary, think about what hardships the American soldiers faced.

December 21. Preparations made for huts. Provisions scarce. . . . Sent a letter to my wife. Heartily wish myself at home. My skin and eyes are almost spoiled with continual smoke. A general cry thro' the camp this evening among the soldiers, "No meat! No meat!" The distant vales echoed back the melancholy sound—"No meat! No meat!" Imitating the noise of crows and owls, also, made a part of the confused music.

"What have you for your dinners, boys?"

"Nothing but fire cake [a flour and water mixture baked over an open fire] and water, Sir."

At night: "Gentlemen, the supper is ready."

"What is your supper, lads?"

"Fire cake and water, Sir."

Very poor beef has been drawn in our camp the greater part of this season. A butcher, bringing a quarter of this kind of beef into camp one day, had white buttons on the knees of his breeches. A soldier cries out, "There, there, Tom, is some more of your fat beef. By my soul I can see the butcher's breeches buttons through it."

December 22. Lay excessive cold and uncomfortable last night. My eyes are started out from their orbits like a rabbit's eyes, occasioned by a great cold and smoke.

"What have you got for breakfast, lads?"

"Fire cake and water, Sir."

The Lord send that our Commissary of Purchases may live [on] fire cake and water till their glutted guts are turned to pasteboard.

Our division are under marching orders this morning. I am ashamed to say it, but I am tempted to steal fowls if I could find them, or even a whole hog, for I feel as if I could eat one. But the impoverished country about us affords but little matter to employ a thief, or keep a clever fellow in good humour. But why do I talk of hunger and hard usage, when so many in the world have not even fire cake and water to eat?

December 25, Christmas. We are still in tents when we ought to be in huts. The poor sick suffer much in tents this cold weather. But we now treat them differently from what they used to be at home under the inspection of old women and Dr. Bolus Linctus. We give them mutton and grog and a capital medicine once in a while to start the disease from its foundation at once. We avoid Piddling Pills, Powders, Bolus's Linctus's Cordials, and all such insignificant matters whose powers are only rendered important by causing the patient to vomit up his money instead of his disease. But very few of the sick men die.

from Albigence Waldo, "Valley Forge, 1777–1778, Diary," *Pennsylvania Magazine of History and Biography*, XXI, No. 3 (1897).

Activity Options

1. Using details from Waldo's diary, visualize what the winter camp at Valley Forge looked like. Draw a sketch to accompany this diary entry and share it with your classmates.

2. Waldo's diary entries provide a vivid portrait of conditions at Valley Forge. Create a chart like this one listing specific sensory details that bring the sights and sounds of Valley Forge to life.

Sights	
Sounds	
Tastes	
Smells	
Touch	

REVIEW CHAPTER 2

Section 3

PRIMARY SOURCE *from* The U.S. Constitution, First Draft

The first draft of the Constitution was printed on August 6, 1787, and submitted to the Constitutional Convention. The copy reprinted below is George Washington's personal copy, which includes his handwritten notes.

WE the People of the States of New-Hampſhire, Maſſachuſetts, Rhode-Iſland and Providence Plantations, Connecticut, New-York, New-Jerſey, Pennſylvania, Delaware, Maryland, Virginia, North-Carolina, South-Carolina, and Georgia, do ordain, declare and eſtabliſh the following Conſtitution for the Government of Ourſelves and our Poſterity.

A R T I C L E   I.

The ſtile of this Government ſhall be, " The United States of America."

II.

The Government ſhall conſiſt of ſupreme legiſlative, executive and judicial powers.

III.

The legiſlative power ſhall be veſted in a Congreſs, to conſiſt of two ſeparate and diſtinct bodies of men, a Houſe of Repreſentatives, and a Senate; ~~each of which ſhall, in all caſes, have a negative on the other.   The Legiſlature ſhall meet on the firſt Monday in December in every year.~~

The Legiſlature ſhall meet at least once in every year and that meeting ſhall be on the firſt Monday in December unleſs a different day ſhall be appointed by law.

IV.

Sect. 1.   The Members of the Houſe of Repreſentatives ſhall be choſen every ſecond year, by the people of the ſeveral States comprehended within this Union. The qualifications of the electors ſhall be the ſame, from time to time, as thoſe of the electors in the ſeveral States, of the moſt numerous branch of their own legiſlatures.

Sect. 2.   Every Member of the Houſe of Repreſentatives ſhall be of the age of twenty-five years at leaſt; ſhall have been a citizen *of* the United States for at leaſt *seven* years before his election; and ſhall be, at the time of his election, *an inhabitant* of the State in which he ſhall be choſen.

Discussion Questions

1. Compare this part of the first draft with the equivalent sections in the final copy printed on page 84 of your textbook. Discuss the major changes that were made in the document in only about five weeks time.

2. What change in the government was emphasized when "We the people of the United States" replaced the listing of the individual states in the Preamble? Why do you think this wording was so important at the time?

REVIEW CHAPTER 2

Section 3

LITERATURE SELECTION *from Legacy*
by James A. Michener

In this excerpt from the novel, young Simon Starr journeys to Philadelphia in 1787 to attend the Constitutional Convention. As you read, pay attention to Simon's impressions of the people he meets there.

On 9 May 1787, when Simon Starr left his family plantation in northern Virginia and started his five-day horseback ride to the Constitutional Convention in Philadelphia, he carried with him the letter of instruction his father had sent from his deathbed in western Massachusetts: ". . . make plans to fill my spot. . . . Fashion a strong new form of government but protect Virginia's interests." More than most delegates, Simon appreciated how difficult it would be to fulfill these two commands.

In the first place, his elders in Virginia had made it clear that he and the other delegates were authorized merely "to correct and improve our present Articles of Confederation, and under no circumstances to meddle with any new form of government." For him to achieve what his father had wanted, a strong central government, would require ignoring these instructions.

In the second place, he realized that a new union could not be established unless the three big states—Massachusetts in the North, with its manufacturing; Pennsylvania in the middle, with its commerce; Virginia in the South, with its tobacco and cotton plantations—found some way to protect their majority interests while ensuring the small states like Rhode Island, New Hampshire and Delaware a respectable voice in whatever form of government emerged. Up to now, it had been one state—one voice, but with the big states constantly accumulating more power and responsibility, such an imbalance could not continue. Rhode Island did not carry the weight of Virginia in population, trade or wealth, and to claim that she did was folly.

He was perplexed as to how this impasse would be resolved, but he was sure of one thing: he would never allow Virginia's rights to be trampled.

Simon was twenty-eight years old that spring, a graduate of the College of New Jersey at Princeton, red-headed, quick to anger, interested in all aspects of American life. He had served as foot soldier in the latter years of the Revolution, rising to the rank of captain, but he had known none of the commanding figures of that period. In recent years, however, he had corresponded with two of the most brilliant men in Virginia or the nation, George Mason and George Wythe, the dazzling professor of law at William and Mary College. Simon was literate, informed, patriotic, and determined to conduct himself with distinction at the Convention.

As he left that May he assured his wife and young son: "I'll be back for the fall harvest," and as he rode down the long lane to the highway, he called out the same message to the slaves who lined the pathway to bid him farewell.

In his compact canvas saddle bags he carried four books he had come to treasure at college: Thucydides' account of the Greek wars, John Locke's treatise on government, a book by Adam Smith on the political economy of nations, a saucy novel by Henry Fielding. In his head he carried about as good an education as was then available in either the United States or Great Britain, but in both Princeton and Virginia he had been careful to mask any pretension to superiority. He was an earnest young man of solid ability who would always show deference to his elders. As one of the two youngest members of the Convention he would feel himself at a disadvantage, but he intended to associate himself with older men of talent and make his contribution through supporting them.

He rode into Philadelphia, a burgeoning city of some forty thousand, in the late afternoon of Sunday, 13 May 1787, and without difficulty he found Market Street, the main east-west thoroughfare, which he pursued toward the Delaware River until he came to Fourth Street. Here, in accordance with instructions, he turned south till he saw ahead, swaying in the evening breeze, the reassuring signboard of the Indian Queen Tavern. He tied his horse, took

> *As one of the two youngest members of the Convention he would feel himself at a disadvantage.*

down his saddle bags, and strode inside to announce himself to the innkeeper: "Simon Starr of Virginia, for the room assigned to my father, Jared Starr."

At the mention of this name, several men who had been idly talking showed great interest and moved forward to meet the newcomer. In the next exciting moments he met members of the Virginia delegation, including four men of distinction: Edmund Randolph, James Madison, and the two older scholars with whom he'd been in correspondence, George Mason and George Wythe. Looking carefully at each as he was introduced, he said: "And General Washington's a Virginian, too. Add him to you gentlemen, and Virginia's to be strongly represented," and Madison said quietly: "We planned it that way."

"I rode hard to get here for tomorrow's opening session," Starr said, to which Madison replied, with a touch of asperity: "No need. There'll be no session."

"Why?" and young Starr learned the first basic fact about the Convention: "Takes seven of the thirteen states to form a legal quorum. Only four are here now."

"When will the others arrive?" and Madison said sourly: "Who knows?"

Eleven days were wasted in idleness as delegates straggled in, and each evening Madison informed those already in attendance of the situation: "Two more states reported today. Perhaps by the end of next week." If the nation was, as the Virginia delegation believed, in peril, the men designated to set it right seemed in no hurry to start.

And shortly, there was sobering news: "Rhode Island has refused to have anything to do with our Convention and will send no delegates." This meant that only twelve states would do the work.

One night during the waiting period Starr returned to the Indian Queen, to see a group of delegates speaking with a newcomer, a slender, handsome, self-contained young man of thirty, so compelling in his manner that Simon whispered to a friend: "Who's that?" and when the man said: "Alexander Hamilton, just in from New York," Starr gasped so loudly that the newcomer turned, gazed at him with penetrating eyes, and said, almost grandly: "Yes?"

"I'm Jared Starr's son."

And now the icy reserve which Hamilton had been showing melted in the sun of remembered friendship. Elbowing his way out of the crowd, he hurried to Simon, embraced him warmly with both arms, and cried: "When I learned of your father's death I felt mortally stricken. A man rarely finds such a trusted friend."

They spent three hours together that first night, with Hamilton probing in a dozen different directions to determine Starr's attitudes, and as the evening waned, it became clear that the two men had even more in common than Hamilton had had with old Jared Starr. Both believed in a strong kind of central government, in the right of large states to exercise large powers, and particularly in the sanctity of property. But toward the end of that first exploration Simon heard several of Hamilton's opinions which could be interpreted as an inclination toward a monarchical form of government: "Simon, the world is divided into those with power and those without. Control of government must rest with the former, because they have most at hazard. Whatever kind of supreme ruler we devise, he should serve for life and so should the members of the stronger house, if we have more than one. That way we avoid the domination of the better class by the poorer."

"Poorer? Do you mean money?"

Hamilton bit his knuckle: "Yes, I suppose I do. But I certainly want those with no money to have an interest in our government. But actually voting? No, no. That should be reserved for those with financial interests to protect."

When Simon accompanied Hamilton to the door of the Indian Queen, he experienced a surge of devotion for this brilliant young man, so learned, so sure of himself, so clear-minded in his vision of what his adopted nation needed: "Father told me that you were the best man he'd ever met, Colonel Hamilton. Tonight I understand why." Then, hesitantly, he added: "If I can help you in the days ahead, please let me know. You can depend on my support."

In the next week, when the delegates chafed because a quorum had still not reached Philadelphia, Simon remained close to his Virginia delegation and watched with what care they laid their plans to assume intellectual and political control of the Convention. The three awesome minds,

> *"Whatever kind of supreme ruler we devise, he should serve for life and so should the members of the stronger house, if we have more than one."*

Mason, Madison, and Wythe, perfected a general plan they had devised for a wholly new government, and it was agreed that at the first opportunity on opening day, the imposing Edmund Randolph would present it as a working paper around which the other delegates would have to frame their arguments. "If we put up a good plan," Madison said, "we'll probably lose two-thirds of the minor details, but the solid structure will still remain."

At the close of the Convention, a hundred and sixteen days later, Simon Starr would draft a perceptive memorandum regarding his major experiences; these notes would not record the great debates or the machinations by which the new government was formed, but they would depict honestly one young man's reactions to the men who gathered in Philadelphia that hot summer, and no entry was more illuminating than his summary of the people involved:

Only twelve states nominated delegates and they authorized a total of 74 men to come to , and of these, only 41 stayed to the bitter end, but of these, only 39 were willing to sign our finished document.

One of his entries that was widely quoted in later years dealt with the composition of the membership, and although the comments on those who were there could have been provided by other observers, his list of those who were conspicuous by their absence was startling:

I was surprised at how many delegates had college degrees like my own. Harvard, Yale, King's College in New York, the College of among them men from Oxford in England, the Inns of Court in London, Utrecht in Holland, and St. Andrews in Scotland. We were not a bunch of illiterate farmers. We were, said some, 'the pick of the former Colonies.'
But I was equally impressed by the luminous names I expected to see in our group and didn't. Patrick Henry was missing and so were the two Adamses from Massachusetts. Tom Jefferson was absent in France. John Marshall wasn't here, nor James Monroe nor John Jay, John Hancock, my father's friend, wasn't here, nor famous Dr. Benjamin Rush. And I expected to see the famous writer and political debater Noah Webster, but he wasn't here.

> **Patrick Henry was missing and so were the two Adamses from Massachusetts. Tom Jefferson was absent in France.**

Eight men were on hand, however, whose presence gave not only Simon Starr but all the other delegates a sense of awe. These were the men who, eleven years before, had dared to sign the Declaration of Independence: these were the men who along with Simon's father had placed their lives in jeopardy to defend the principle of freedom. One by one, these eight introduced themselves to Simon, reminding him of the high esteem in which his father had been held, and he was deeply moved by the experience. Two of the veterans earned a special place in his affections:

I was disappointed on opening day to find that Benjamin Franklin was not present, but on the morning of the second day I heard a commotion in the street outside our meeting hall and some cheering. Running to glimpse what might be happening, I saw coming down the middle of the street an amazing sight, a glassed-in ornate sedan chair of the kind used by European kings. It hung suspended from two massive poles which rested on the shoulders of eight huge prisoners from the local jail. Inside, perched on pillows, rode an old, baldheaded man who looked like a jolly bullfrog. It was Dr. Franklin, most eminent of the delegates, and the oldest at eighty-one. Gout, obesity and creaking joints made it impossible for him to walk, hence the sedan chair. When the prisoners carried him into the hall, someone alerted him that I was present. Calling "Halt!" to the prisoners, he beckoned me to approach, and when I did he reached out with both hands to embrace me, and tears came into his eyes: "Son of a brave man, be like him."

Research Options

1. A historical novel takes its setting and some of its characters and events from history. Find out which characters in this excerpt are fictional and which actually lived. Then make a list of historical figures and compare it with those of your classmates.

2. Investigate the real-life story of one of the historical figures on your list. Then write a brief biographical sketch about this person. Work with your classmates to create a *Who's Who of the Constitutional Convention.*

AMERICAN LIVES ## Haym Salomon
Financier of the Revolution

"The kindness of [Haym Salomon] . . . will preserve me from extremities . . . [but] he obstinately rejects all recompense."—James Madison (1782)

Haym Salomon spent little over a decade in America, but he chose a crucial time and played a vital role. From 1778 until his death in 1785, he helped raise funds for the Continental Congress and made loans to many members of the army and government. He was owed large sums by the government he aided—sums never repaid.

Salomon was born around 1740 in Poland. He supported independence for that land, which suffered partition by other, stronger powers. In 1772 he left Poland for London and soon after arrived in New York. He joined in the agitation for American independence and in the fall of 1776 was arrested by British authorities as a spy. They soon released him, however, preferring to use him as an interpreter: because he knew German, he could communicate with Hessian mercenaries. Unknown to the British, Salomon acted as a double agent by persuading Hessians to desert. About this time, Salomon married.

In 1778 Salomon was arrested again, charged with joining a plot to burn the British fleet and warehouses. Condemned to death, he managed to escape by bribing his guard. He fled south, leaving his wife and an infant son behind. Reaching Philadelphia, Salomon sent a letter to the Continental Congress explaining his actions on behalf of the cause and requesting a job. None came, but with the help of local Jewish business people, he began a business in finance.

Over the next few years, Salomon—along with other Jewish merchants—helped Robert Morris finance the Revolution. He sold bonds issued by Congress, getting valuable Dutch and French money in return. By taking a small commission—only a quarter of one percent—he pleased Congress, which named him official broker of United States bonds. He was also named official paymaster for the French army in the United States and handled virtually all of the money that the Dutch gave the colonies' struggling cause.

Salomon also assisted a number of important actors in the revolutionary cause. His loans—often

with no interest charged—to James Madison prompted the praise quoted above. He loaned money as well to Thomas Jefferson, James Wilson, and Edmund Randolph, all members of Congress. He also made loans to Baron Friedrich von Steuben, General Thaddeus Kosciuszko, and General Arthur St. Clair.

Salomon, though new to the colonies, tried to make the United States a welcome home for future Jewish immigration. In 1783 he joined with another Philadelphia Jew in asking the government of Pennsylvania to change a part of its constitution. The constitution required that new members of the state assembly "acknowledge the Scriptures of the Old and New Testament." Salomon and his colleague pointed out that this oath would exclude Jews, which they argued was unfair given the contribution that the Jewish community had made. While the request was denied at the time, a new state constitution was adopted six years later that cut the oath. In 1784, a financier in Philadelphia criticized Jewish moneylenders for charging high rates. Salomon wrote a defense of the Jewish contribution to the cause of independence.

Early the next year, though, Salomon died, though he was only in his mid-forties. His health may have suffered from his imprisonment by the British. When he died, he was bankrupt, suffering from the lack of repayment of private as well as public loans. His family later claimed that the United States owed him almost $660,000. The exact amount is not known, as Salomon did not keep good records. While a Congressional committee in 1864 acknowledged that the claim had "undeniable merit," it was never repaid.

Questions

1. What principles of the Revolution would appeal to Salomon and other Jewish people?
2. Describe Salomon's contribution to the revolutionary cause.
3. Why did Salomon feel the need to defend the contribution of Jews to the Revolution?

REVIEW CHAPTER 2

Section 3

AMERICAN LIVES Patrick Henry
Passionate Orator Full of Contradictions

*"Here is a revolution as radical as that which separated us from Great Britain. . . .
Our rights and privileges are endangered, and the sovereignty of the states . . .
relinquished."—Patrick Henry, speech against ratification of the Constitution (1788)*

In 1775, Patrick Henry spoke passionately for independence: "I know not what course others may take; but as for me . . . give me liberty or give me death!" In 1788, he also spoke passionately against the new Constitution: "It is said eight states have adopted this plan. I declare that if twelve states and a half had adopted it, I would with manly firmness, and in spite of an erring world, reject it." Henry's oratory propelled him to a major role in Virginia and national politics, but his vivid speech-making often revealed contradictions.

Patrick Henry (1736–1799) failed in two attempts to become a merchant and chose a career in law. He relied on his intelligence and speaking skill to pass the bar exam. He became a successful lawyer, gaining wealth and some fame throughout Virginia. He soon entered politics.

Henry joined Virginia's House of Burgesses in May 1765 as the Stamp Act became an issue. He quickly shattered custom—new members were supposed to sit and watch—by introducing resolutions condemning the act. One said that the Burgesses, not Parliament, had the "sole exclusive right and power to lay taxes" in Virginia. Speaking in their favor, Henry compared King George III to rulers who had been overthrown. The assembly erupted in angry cries of "treason!"

In 1774, Virginia sent Henry and six others to Philadelphia as delegates to the First Continental Congress. His main contribution was, typically, a stirring speech urging united action: "The distinctions between Virginians, Pennsylvanians, New Yorkers and New Englanders are no more. I am not a Virginian, but an American." Back in Virginia, Henry again offered bold resolutions. They said that Virginia should "be immediately put into a position of defense" and "prepare a plan" for creating and arming a military force. Here he gave his famous "liberty or death" speech.

During the Revolution, Henry focused on Virginia politics, serving as governor five times. Hoping to secure Virginia's claim to western lands,

he sent George Rogers Clark with an armed force to Illinois territory to drive out the British. During this period, he and Thomas Jefferson began a feud that lasted the rest of Henry's life. Henry feuded with James Madison as well. These personal quarrels soon had an impact on politics.

While Henry was governor, John Jay negotiated a treaty with Spain that gave up American rights to trade on the Mississippi River. Henry—who felt the loss of trade would weaken Virginia's power—was infuriated. From then on he opposed national power.

This position—and the feud with Madison—came together when the Constitution was submitted to the states for approval. Henry spoke for 18 of Virginia's 23 days of debate. He objected to the lack of a guarantee of individual rights, and his objection is credited with the Bill of Rights being added to the Constitution. However, contradicting his words of 1774, Henry also objected because Virginia would lose power under a federal system: "This government is not a Virginian, but an American government." In the end, Virginia voted to ratify the Constitution. But Henry used his influence to get Antifederalists named as Virginia's two senators, denying James Madison a seat in the first Senate.

After the defeat, Henry retired for a time. Ironically, his last public role came in support of the Federalist Party—which Jefferson and Madison now opposed. The year he died, Henry, the great Antifederalist, was elected to Congress as a candidate of the Federalist party.

Questions

1. What contradictory stands did Henry take?
2. What actions and positions of Henry reveal concern with Virginia's power?
3. Support the argument that Henry should be as well know for his insistence on a Bill of Rights for the Constitution as for his "liberty or death" speech.

Name _____ Date _____

GUIDED READING *Preamble and Article 1*

As you read the Preamble and Article 1 of the Constitution, answer the questions below. Circle **Yes** or **No** for each question and provide the location of the information that supports your answer. All information is in Article 1, so you need to supply only the section and clause information. Section 4, Clause 2 would be written 4.2.

                                                                        Yes (No)

Example: Do states have varying numbers of Senators? _____ Location   *3I*

1. Lois Deevers, a Texan for two years, is 26 years old and has been a U.S. citizen for ten years. Could she serve as a congresswoman from Texas?   Yes No Location _____

2. Ky Pham is 32 years old and became a U.S. citizen at the age of 24. Could he serve as a senator from Maine, where he has lived his entire life?   Yes No Location _____

3. If the Senate votes 49 to 49 on a bill, does the President of the Senate cast the tie-breaking vote?   Yes No Location _____

4. Can a senator be sued for slander because of things he or she said in a speech on the floor of the Senate?   Yes No Location _____

5. If Congress creates a new government agency, can a senator or representative resign from office to become the head of that agency?   Yes No Location _____

6. Can the Senate expel one of its members?   Yes No Location _____

7. If the House unanimously votes to override a presidential veto, and the Senate votes to override by a vote of 64 to 34, does the bill become law?   Yes No Location _____

8. Can Congress pass an *ex post facto* law if both houses favor it by a two-thirds majority?   Yes No Location _____

9. Can a state impose an import tax on goods entering from another state?   Yes No Location _____

10. Could a bill pass the Senate by a vote of 26 to 27?   Yes No Location _____

11. If a bill is sent to the president one week before Congress adjourns, and the president neither signs it nor returns it, does it become law?   Yes No Location _____

12. Can a state legally engage in war with a foreign nation if the state is invaded by troops of that nation?   Yes No Location _____

GUIDED READING *Articles 2 and 3*

As you read Articles 2 and 3, answer each of the following questions by writing **Yes** or **No** on the blank line. Each question is specifically answered by the Constitution.

Article 2

_____ 1. Is the length of a president's term set by the Constitution?

_____ 2. Does the number of electors that each state has in the Electoral College vary from state to state?

_____ 3. Must national elections be held in November?

_____ 4. Can a 30-year-old, natural-born citizen hold the office of president?

_____ 5. Can an 80-year-old person who became a U.S. citizen at the age of 21 hold the office of president?

_____ 6. Does a president's salary always remain the same while in office?

_____ 7. Must someone elected to the presidency take an oath before taking office?

_____ 8. Can the president pardon someone convicted of treason?

_____ 9. Must the president report to Congress about how the nation is doing?

_____ 10. Can a president convicted of bribery remain in office?

Article 3

_____ 11. Can a president dismiss a member of the Supreme Court and replace him or her with someone more in agreement with the president?

_____ 12. Can the salary paid to a federal judge be lowered while that judge remains in office?

_____ 13. Must a case in which a resident of Nebraska sues a citizen of Louisiana be heard in a federal court?

_____ 14. Can someone who publicly urges others to overthrow the federal government be convicted of treason for that position?

_____ 15. Can a person who gives secret information about U.S. military plans to a foreign government be convicted of treason?

_____ 16. Can a person who denies having committed treason be convicted on the testimony of a single person who witnessed the treasonous act?

GUIDED READING *Articles 4–7*

As you read Articles 4–7, answer the following questions and note the article (with section and clause, when necessary) that is the source for the relevant information. Article 4, Section 3, Clause 2 would be written 4.3.2.

                                                                                                    Yes (No)
Example: Could Utah refuse to allow a U.S. citizen from Ohio to buy a home in Utah?   Location   _42_

Article 4

                                                                                                    Yes   No
1. Must one state honor the ruling of a state court in another state? ....   Location _____

2. If a woman commits a crime in Kentucky and is captured in New York, can New   Yes   No
   York refuse to return her to Kentucky? ....   Location _____

3. Would it be possible for North and South Dakota to become one state if both state   Yes   No
   legislatures, and Congress, approved of such a merger? ....   Location _____

4. Can one state establish a dictatorship within that state as long as it does not   Yes   No
   interfere with the lives of citizens in other states? ....   Location _____

Article 5

5. What institution decides when an amendment to the Constitution should be   Answer   _____
   proposed and considered? ....   Location _____

                                                                                     Answer   _____
6. How many states must approve an amendment for it to take effect? ....   Location _____

Article 6
                                                                                                    Yes   No
7. Can one state enforce a law within its own borders that conflicts with a
   national law? ....   Location _____

8. If a man refused to support the Constitution, could he serve as a member of his   Yes   No
   state's legislature? ....   Location _____

                                                                                                    Yes   No
9. Can an atheist be denied the right to hold federal office? ....   Location _____

Article 7
10. How many states had to ratify the Constitution for it to become the law of the   Answer   _____
    land? ....   Location _____

11. In what year was the Constitution signed by delegates to the Constitutional   Answer   _____
    Convention? ....   Location _____

Name _____ Date _____

GUIDED READING *The Amendments*

As you read the amendments to the Constitution, circle the correct choice from each parenthetical pair of choices in the summary below.

Amendment 1   establishes the people's right to (vote/criticize the government).
Amendment 2   maintains that states have the right to have (armed militias/legislatures).
Amendment 3   protects people from being forced to (serve as/house) soldiers in peacetime.
Amendment 4   requires police to provide a (good reason/written accusation) to obtain a search warrant.
Amendment 5   guarantees that the government cannot take private property for its own use without (the owner's agreement/fair payment).
Amendment 6   protects the rights of (crime victims/people accused of crimes).
Amendment 7   requires that most people accused of civil crimes be given a (jury/speedy) trial.
Amendment 8   says that bails, fines, and punishments for crimes cannot be (delayed/unfair or cruel).
Amendment 9   states that people's rights (are/are not) limited to those listed in the Constitution.
Amendment 10   says that government powers not mentioned in the Constitution belong to (the states or the people/the House of Representatives).
Amendment 11   prohibits a citizen of one state from suing another (state/citizen) in a federal court.
Amendment 12   requires that electors for president and vice president clearly identify (the party each candidate belongs to/the person they choose for each office).
Amendment 13   forbids slavery in the (South/United States).
Amendment 14   requires that states give all people (the right to vote/equal protection under the law).
Amendment 15   prohibits denying voting rights because of (sex/race).
Amendment 16   establishes Congress's right to pass (an income/a sales) tax.
Amendment 17   changes the way in which (the president/U.S. senators) are elected.
Amendment 18   establishes (prohibition/civil rights).
Amendment 19   prohibits denying the right to vote based on (age/sex).
Amendment 20   (shortens/lengthens) the time between elections and taking office.
Amendment 21   repeals Amendment (17/18).
Amendment 22   limits the (years/number) of presidential terms.
Amendment 23   gives residents of Washington, D.C., the right to vote in (presidential/local) elections.
Amendment 24   forbids a tax on (voting/property).
Amendment 25   establishes when and how the (Speaker of the House/vice-president) can take over presidential powers.
Amendment 26   extends suffrage to (residents/citizens) who are 18 years of age.
Amendment 27   deals with pay raises for (members of Congress/the president).

Name _____   Date _____

BUILDING VOCABULARY *The Constitution*

A. Completion Select the term or name that best completes the sentence.

electoral college   judicial review
legislative   judiciary
elastic clause   executive
amendments   preamble

1. The Constitution's opening statement, which explains its purpose, is known as the _____.

2. The House of Representatives and the Senate comprise the _____ branch of government.

3. The system used for electing the president of the United States is known as the _____.

4. _____ is the implied power of the Supreme Court to declare laws unconstitutional.

5. Clauses added to the Constitution to address specific issues are known as _____.

B. Matching Match the definition in the second column with the term or terms in the first column. Write the appropriate letter next to the word.

_____ 1. executive   a. presidential rejection of a bill

_____ 2. Bill of Rights   b. the act of officially adopting

_____ 3. impeach   c. provision giving Congress implied powers

_____ 4. veto   d. branch headed by the U.S. president

_____ 5. elastic clause   e. first ten amendments

_____ 6. ratification   f. to accuse an official of wrongdoing

C. Writing Write a paragraph summarize several key amendments using the following terms:

search and seizure   speedy and public trial   poll tax

Name _____ Date _____

SKILLBUILDER PRACTICE *Clarifying; Summarizing*

Discussion of search warrants and warrants to arrest a person are commonly heard on police and detective television programs. The need for such warrants is based in Amendment 4 of the Bill of Rights. Read the Amendment, then fill in the charts below to help clarify the language of this important protection of citizens' rights. Use a dictionary, if you like. (See Skillbuilder Handbook, p. 914.)

Amendment 4. Search and Seizure The right of the people to be secure in their persons, houses, papers, and effects, against unreasonable searches and seizures, shall not be violated, and no warrants shall issue, but upon probable cause, supported by oath or affirmation, and particularly describing the place to be searched, and the persons or things to be seized.

Original word or phrase	How you would define it
1. secure	1.
2. effects	2.
3. seizure	3.
4. warrant	4.
5. issue	5.
6. probable cause	6.
7. affirmation	7.

8. Original wording: The right of the people to be secure in their persons, houses, papers, and effects, against unreasonable searches and seizures, shall not be violated . . .

Simplified wording:

9. Original wording: . . . and no warrants shall issue, but upon probable cause, supported by oath or affir- mation, and particularly describing the place to be searched, and the persons or things to be seized.

Simplified wording:

RETEACHING ACTIVITY *The Constitution*

Article 1

Complete the following sentences with the word or words that fit best.

revenue	elastic
Senate	two-thirds
two	six
House of Representatives	president
money	impeachment
commerce	

1. The legislative branch is composed of two bodies, the _____ and the

_____ .

2. Among the expressed powers of Congress are the power to collect _____,

borrow _____, and regulate _____ .

3. The _____ clause gives Congress the authority to perform acts not specifically

stated in the Constitution.

4. The Vice-President of the United States is the _____ of the Senate, but may

not vote on legislation unless the Senate is tied.

5. The House of Representatives has the sole power of _____, but it is the

Senate's duty to try all accused officials.

6. Congress may pass a law over the president's veto with a _____ vote in each

house.

7. Elections for the House of Representatives are held every _____ years, while

elections for the Senate are held every _____years.

RETEACHING ACTIVITY *The Constitution*

Articles 2 & 3

Write *T* in the blank space if the sentence is true or *F* is the sentence is false. If the sentence is false, rewrite to make it true.

_____ 1. No person except a natural born citizen who has reached the age of 35 and has

been a resident of the United States for at least 14 years may run for president.

_____

_____ 2. The Speaker of the House of Representatives is the first in line to succeed the

president should he or she become unable to perform the duties of the office.

_____

_____ 3. The president may make treaties with foreign nations without approval from

Congress.

_____

_____ 3. Congress has the power to remove a president from office through an

impeachment and conviction.

_____

_____ 5. The Supreme Court is the final court of appeal in the United States.

_____

_____ 6. Justices to the Supreme Court are appointed by Congress.

_____

Name _____ Date _____

RETEACHING ACTIVITY *The Constitution*

Articles 4–7

A. Explain how the Constitution solves each problem listed below.

Problem	Problem
1. A major U.S. city is the scene of domestic violence, and many people in the state are in danger. _____ _____ Solution _____ _____	2. A person is charged with a serious crime in one state and flees to another state. _____ _____ Solution _____ _____

B. Explain the procedures for amending the Constitution.

   3. Proposing Amendments: _____

   _____

   4. Ratifying Amendments: _____

   _____

C. Answer the following questions.

   5. What type of test shall never be required as a qualification to any public office in the

   United States? _____

   6. How many states had to ratify the Constitution before it could go into effect?

   _____

   7. In what year was the Constitution signed by the delegates to the Constitutional

   Convention? _____

RETEACHING ACTIVITY *The Constitution*

The Amendments

Choose the best answer for each item. Write the letter of your answer on the blank.

_____ 1. The first ten amendments to the Constitution are known as the
   a. preamble.
   b. Articles of Confederation.
   c. Bill of Rights.
   d. Fundamental Orders.

_____ 2. The First Amendment guarantees the right to
   a. bear arms.
   b. free speech.
   c. privacy.
   d. vote.

_____ 3. The Twelfth Amendment was the result of the presidential election of
   a. 1792.
   b. 1796.
   c. 1800.
   d. 1804.

_____ 4. The Thirteenth Amendment abolished
   a. the slave trade.
   b. indentured servitude.
   c. lynching.
   d. slavery.

_____ 5. A citizen's right to vote is guaranteed by the
   a. First Amendment.
   b. Fourth Amendment.
   c. Fourteenth Amendment.
   d. Fifteenth Amendment.

_____ 6. The Nineteenth Amendment gave women
   a. the right to vote.
   b. the right to bear arms.
   c. equal pay in the workplace.
   d. equal access to education

_____ 7. The Twenty-second Amendment limits a president to
   a. one term in office.
   b. two terms in office.
   c. three terms in office.
   d. four terms in office.

_____ 8. The Twenty-sixth Amendment lowered the voting age to
   a. 17.
   b. 18.
   c. 19.
   d. 20.

Name _____   Date _____

GEOGRAPHY APPLICATION: REGION *The Electoral College*

Directions: Read the paragraphs below and study the map carefully. Then answer the questions that follow.

Delegates to the Constitutional Convention of 1787 debated the question of presidential election. Some wanted direct election. Others favored election by Congress. They compromised on a plan of indirect election by electors picked by popular vote. Called the electoral college, the plan is a double-election system.

Here is how it works. Political parties in each state choose electors, people pledged to support a party's candidate. The number of electors for each party equals the combined number of that state's U.S. senators and representatives. (Today there are 535 U.S. senators and representatives, plus 3 electors from the District of Columbia, for a national total of 538 electors.) A candidate must have a majority to win. Then, if no one receives 270 electors' votes, the House of Representatives chooses a winner from the top three vote getters.

On election day, citizens vote for president. Their votes, however, are actually for electors pledged to that person. The candidate getting the majority of popular votes gets all the electoral votes of the state.

Then, about six weeks after the election, electors meet at their state capitals to cast ballots directly for president. But this may not mirror the country's popular vote. If, for example, someone gets a small majority in a few states with a big electoral count but loses heavily in many small states, a minority of nationwide popular votes can control a majority of electoral votes. In fact, four times—1824, 1876, 1888 and 2000—a candidate not having the largest popular vote became president through the electoral college.

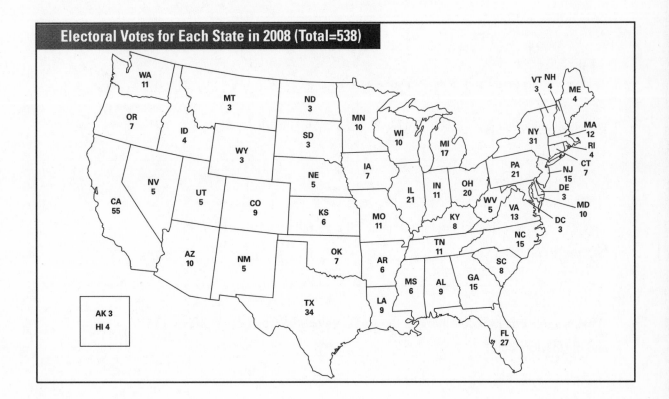

Electoral Votes for Each State in 2008 (Total=538)

WA 11
MT 3
ND 3
MN 10
VT 3
NH 4
ME 4
OR 7
ID 4
WY 3
SD 3
WI 10
MI 17
NY 31
MA 12
RI 4
CT 7
NV 5
UT 5
CO 9
NE 5
IA 7
IL 21
IN 11
OH 20
PA 21
NJ 15
DE 3
CA 55
KS 6
MO 11
KY 8
WV 5
VA 13
MD 10
DC 3
AZ 10
NM 5
OK 7
AR 6
TN 11
NC 15
SC 8
TX 34
LA 9
MS 6
AL 9
GA 15
FL 27
AK 3
HI 4

Interpreting Text and Visuals

1. How was the electoral process for choosing the president decided on at the
   Constitutional Convention? _____

   _____

   _____

2. How is the number of electoral votes for each state determined? _____

   _____

   _____

3. What do you think caused some delegates to the Constitutional Convention of
   1787 to be unwilling to let the people elect the president directly? _____

   _____

   _____

4. Which six states and one district have the fewest electoral votes? How many does
   each have? _____

   _____

   How many electoral votes does your state have? _____

5. How does the electoral college's "double-election" system work? _____

   _____

   _____

6. Explain how a presidential candidate can lose the overall popular vote and still
   become president. _____

   _____

7. What possible criticism do you see of the six-week delay between the popular vote
   and the electors' vote? _____

   _____

   _____

AMERICAN LIVES James Madison
Quiet Politician

"Every person seems to acknowledge his greatness. He blends together the profound politician, with the Scholar. In the management of every great question he evidently took the lead in the Convention."—William Pierce, Georgia delegate to the Constitutional Convention, on James Madison (1787)

James Madison was an unlikely politician. Frail, a hypochondriac, and shy, he was a private person who did not like campaigning and spoke so softly he was not always heard. Yet he served more than 40 years in public office, impressing people with his learning and careful preparation.

An eager student, Madison (1751–1836) read every book in his father's library by age eleven. After studying with a tutor, he attended the College of New Jersey (now Princeton) and completed a three-year course in two years. After one more year of study, he returned home, suffering a physical or emotional breakdown.

He was energized to enter politics when he met some Baptists imprisoned for their religious beliefs. Madison vowed to help them. In 1776, he joined the Virginia Convention and won approval of a call for the "free exercise of religion."

From 1776 to 1787, Madison served either in Virginia's revolutionary government or the national Congress. He won another victory for religious freedom, persuading the Virginia assembly to pass a law that ended the Anglican Church's status as an official religion. Throughout this period, he concluded that the Confederation government was too weak to be effective.

Madison prepared for the Constitutional Convention by reading the history of other confederations. He listed their weaknesses and drafted the outlines of a new constitution. His ideas formed the basis of what was submitted as the Virginia Plan. Madison attended virtually every minute of the sessions, taking notes of the proceedings. He spoke often, always in defense of a strong central government. He also argued strongly for direct election of the legislature, which he called vital "to every plan of free government."

Madison wrote about a third of the *Federalist Papers* urging ratification of the new Constitution. Critics argued that the document gave the new government power to tyrannize over individuals. Madison tried to reassure them: "Justice is the end

of government. . . . It ever has been, and ever will be pursued, until it be obtained or until liberty be lost in the pursuit." During June 1788, he debated Patrick Henry, using his greater learning to combat Henry's more passionate appeals. Madison won, and Virginia ratified the Constitution. Yet Henry, who controlled the Virginia Assembly, succeeded in denying Madison either of the state's seats in the new Senate. He also tried to draw a district boundary that would prevent Madison from winning a seat in the House, but Madison did win election.

The Constitution was approved in part because of the promise to enact a Bill of Rights. Some wanted a new convention to draft these amendments, but Madison feared that such a meeting would rewrite the whole Constitution, undoing all the careful work. So, he wrote the necessary amendments and pushed the first Congress to pass them and send them to the states for final approval. Thus, a new convention was not needed.

Madison went on to serve as his friend Thomas Jefferson's secretary of state for eight years and as president for another eight. He left office in 1817 scarred by divisions in the country caused by the War of 1812. In his remaining 19 years, Madison grew alarmed at the increasing divisions between sections. When he died, a brief message called "Advice to My Country" was discovered. It said: "The advice nearest to my heart and deepest in my convictions is, that the Union of the States be cherished and preserved." It was a union that he had done much to build.

Questions

1. Is a person of Madison's shyness likely to succeed in politics now? Explain your answer.
2. What did Madison do to promote religious freedom?
3. In what sense is it fair to call Madison the "father of the Constitution"?

AMERICAN LIVES # Thurgood Marshall
Lawyer, Jurist, Crusader for Equality

"Cast aside today are those condemned to face society's ultimate penalty. Tomorrow's victims may be minorities, women, or the indigent. Inevitably [these rulings] . . . will squander the authority and legitimacy of this court as a protector of the powerless."—Thurgood Marshall, dissenting opinion in **Payne v. Tennessee (1991)**

Born the great-grandson of a slave, Thurgood Marshall (1908–1993) did as much as anyone to erase the legacy of slavery. As a lawyer and as a Supreme Court justice, he fought to ensure that African Americans had full equality before the law.

Marshall was born to a middle-class African-American family of Baltimore. He was a spirited child who frequently suffered his elementary school principal's favorite punishment: being sent to the school's basement to memorize part of the Constitution. "Before I left that school," Marshall later recalled, "I knew the Constitution by heart."

After graduation from college, he applied to the University of Maryland law school but was turned down because of his race. He attended the Howard University Law School instead—graduating with high honors—and joined the Baltimore chapter of the National Association for the Advancement of Colored People (NAACP). Soon he won his first case: a suit against the Maryland law school that had refused to enroll him. It was, he later said, "sweet revenge."

Within a few years, Marshall had joined the NAACP's national Legal Defense Fund, which he was named to head in 1938. From that position, he began to chip away at segregation, especially in education. Marshall's workload was tremendous: by the mid-1950s, he handled 50 court cases a year and traveled 60,000 miles a year preparing and arguing his cases. He argued 32 cases before the Supreme Court—and won 29. Most prominent was the 1954 decision *Brown* v. *Board of Education*. In past education cases, Marshall had won Court agreement that African Americans should receive equal access to postgraduate or professional education. In *Brown*, Marshall used the Fourteenth and Fifteenth Amendments to attack segregated public schools. In oral arguments, he put the issue bluntly: the Court should "strike down all types" of laws treating people differently according to race. To justify segregation, "there would have to be some

recognition of a reason why of all the multitudinous groups of people in this country you have to single out Negroes and give them this special treatment." There was, he went on, no such reason. The Court ruled unanimously that segregation in education was unconstitutional. Marshall was "so happy I was numb."

Marshall soon went back to work, trying to ensure that school systems complied with the Court. In 1961, he was named a judge of the U.S. Court of Appeals. He did not wish to abandon the cause of civil rights, but felt that the Legal Defense Fund had an able staff and that duty called. In four years as a judge and two years as solicitor general of the United States, Marshall became an effective advocate for citizen's rights. In 1967, President Lyndon Johnson named Marshall as an Associate Justice of the Supreme Court—replacing, ironically, the grandson of a former Confederate soldier.

Marshall served as a justice for almost 25 years. He worked to protect the rights of women and minorities and the right of free speech; he argued frequently to end the death penalty. His views were often expressed in dissenting opinions, as he spent most of his tenure as part of a liberal minority on a conservative Court. His writing reflected a deep understanding of the law and down-to-earth life experience. He was also well known for his humor. When he retired in 1991, he was asked why. "I'm getting old and falling apart," he wryly replied.

Questions

1. In naming Marshall to the Court, Johnson said "he has already earned his place in history." Do you agree or disagree? Explain.
2. How does the *Brown* case show the flexibility of the Constitution?
3. The opening quotation comes from Marshall's last opinion, a dissent in a death penalty case. How does it reflect his concerns as a justice?

Name _____ Date _____

UNiT
1
Project 1

PROJECTS FOR CITIZENSHIP *Becoming an Educated Voter:*
Endorsing a Political Candidate

WRITING A JOB DESCRIPTION Find out the requirements for the elective office
you have chosen. The requirements for the president and for members of Congress
can be found in the Constitution. Requirements for members of state government
can be found in state constitutions. For local offices, check with your city hall, town
clerk, or civic organizations such as the League of Women Voters.

Next, make a list of responsibilities for the elective office. What tasks will the
official be expected to perform? What skills would be useful for a candidate to have?

Once you have compiled this information, present it in the form of a job description. The description should present the minimum requirements for the job, the basic
job functions, and useful skills.

STUDYING THE CANDIDATES Next, study the candidates for the office that you
have chosen. Follow the steps in "Learning about the candidates" on page 112 of the
textbook. Present your findings in the form of a resumé—or education-and-work history—for each candidate. Use the following list of topics as a model.

> Name:
>
> Birth Date:
>
> Birthplace:
>
> Education:
>
> Employment History:
>
> Skills and Talents:
>
> Notable Achievements:
>
> Political Philosophy:
>
> Stand on Key Issues:

Compare the candidates' resumés to the job description you wrote. Which candidate do you feel best fulfills the job requirements of the office? Which candidate has
taken political stands with which you agree?

WRITING YOUR ENDORSEMENT Write a political endorsement for the candidate
of your choice. Think of the endorsement as an open letter to the voters in your area.
• Begin your letter with the words, "Dear Voters of [town, city, county, state, etc.]."
• Present the credentials and experience that the candidate will bring to the office.
• Give your own personal reasons for supporting the candidate—that is, the issues
  that you think your candidate addresses most successfully.
• End your letter by summing up the reasons voters should support this candidate.
• Close with the words, "Sincerely, [your name and address]."

UNIT 1
Project 2

PROJECTS FOR CITIZENSHIP *Expressing Political Opinions:*
Writing a Letter to the Editor

PREPARING TO WRITE Before writing your letter, look at the publication you are writing to for any rules governing letters to the editor. The requirements are usually printed at the end of the letters column. They will look something like this.

> The *Morning News* welcomes letters of opinion. Send all letters to Letters to the Editor, Morning News, at the address shown below. Letters must be signed and labeled with your name, address and telephone number. If we print your letter, it may be shortened for space. Your name may be withheld upon request.

WRITING YOUR LETTER When you write your letter (as described in "Writing a persuasive letter" on page 113 of your textbook) keep in mind the following practical suggestions.

✔ **Be neat.** If possible, type your letter. If you can't type or do not have access to a typewriter or computer, write the letter neatly in dark ink.

✔ **Keep it short and simple.** Long-winded letters won't impress an editor. Even short letters may be edited for clarity. Here's a sample letter to a school newspaper that makes its point in very little space.

> *We all support the Tigers, but there's a limit. Do we really need to splash our mascot all over the bridge? Let's think of better ways to get our message across. Go, Tigers!*
>
> Mollie Wilson, sophomore

✔ **Organize your letter clearly.** State the subject of your letter right away. Then give your opinion.

✔ **Keep it civil.** Don't make accusations or statements about anyone else, especially when they may be untrue.

✔ **Support your opinion** with facts and arguments.

✔ **Concentrate on solutions.** If you've pointed out a problem, present a solution or urge readers to take action.

✔ **Proofread your letter.** Fix any mistakes and take out inappropriate language. You might ask a friend to act as editor, providing suggestions for cutting or improving the letter.

✔ **Sign the letter.** Be sure to add any other identifying information the editor requires. If you don't want your name printed with the letter, explain why. Your letter, if printed, will end with the words "name withheld."

A letter on a topic of current interest, especially one recently covered by the newspaper or magazine, will have the best chance of being published.

Name _____ Date _____

UNIT 1
Project 4

PROJECTS FOR CITIZENSHIP *Volunteering in Your Community: Making an Oral Report*

BECOMING A VOLUNTEER Use the ideas under "Suggestions for volunteering" on page 115 of your textbook to identify the kind of volunteer position you would like to fill.

- **Ask yourself some questions.** Do you like to work face-to-face with people? Organize records? Maintain equipment? Talk on the telephone?
- **Decide how much time you can give** and what hours you can work.
- **Contact an organization** that uses volunteers. Discuss the kinds of tasks you feel qualified to do and interested in doing. Tell them what hours you can work.
- **Do the job conscientiously.** Once you accept a volunteer position, think of it as you would any job. Arrive on time. Give it your best effort.
- **Keep a journal of your experiences.** Make notes that answer the following questions: What surprised you about the job? What was the hardest part? Did you enjoy it? What was the best thing about the job? Would you do it again? Would you recommend it to others?
- **If possible, take pictures.** Ask the volunteer organization for permission to photograph the setting and your work.
- **Collect publications.** Keep organization publications—public relations material, such as brochures, news clippings, and so on—as references.

PREPARING YOUR ORAL REPORT Review your journal and the publications you have collected. Write down funny or touching anecdotes you might want to share with the class. Outline your presentation using headings that tell the story (for instance, My First Day and How I Solved a Thorny Problem). Jot down details you remember about the people and tasks you performed. Did you learn any new skills? Did you meet interesting people? Tell about them.

MAKING YOUR ORAL PRESENTATION Once you have written your talk, you need to deliver it to the class. Following are some tips for holding audience attention.

- ✔ Start to talk only when your audience is ready to listen.
- ✔ Speak in a normal voice, but in a tone that is loud enough for everyone to hear.
- ✔ Stick to the subject.
- ✔ Explain any unfamiliar or unusual words.
- ✔ Try to avoid saying "umm" too much, or stringing together your sentences with "ands."
- ✔ Provide new facts and anecdotes that give the audience a fresh perspective on a topic.
- ✔ Refer to your notes, but try not to read from them.
- ✔ Look around the room; encourage questions or comments from the audience.
- ✔ If the audience wants to know more about a topic, expand it. If people start to fidget, personalize the account with an anecdote or switch to a new topic.

The Living Constitution 75

UNIT 1

Project 3

PROJECTS FOR CITIZENSHIP *Understanding How to Lobby: Planning a Lobbying Campaign*

LEARNING THE RULES Before beginning your lobbying campaign, contact the state capital or a civic group such as the League of Women Voters to find out the rules for lobbying in your state. It's a good idea to look for a sponsor, a local legislator or political activist, who will guide your activities or make a staff member available to you.

BUILDING A COALITION One way to strengthen your message is to form a coalition, or working alliance, with others who share your views. Find out the names of people or groups who might be sympathetic to your campaign. For example, if you are working for a law supporting educational reform, you might approach members of the PTA or student governments in other school districts.

CARRYING OUT YOUR LOBBYING PLAN Follow the suggestions under "Creating a lobbying plan" on page 115 in your textbook. Once you have established your goals and done your research, you will be ready to take the following steps.

- **Plan your attack.** Identify different strategies for lobbying, and try as many of these approaches as possible. You can lobby lawmakers in person or by telephone, letter, or e-mail. You also lobby by testifying before a group or committee.
- **Prepare to state your position quickly and clearly.** Create supporting evidence or documentation as necessary. Use a graph or table to summarize data that might otherwise take pages to present.
- **Circulate a petition.** Petitions have an especially big impact. Every signature represents a potential vote. You might use the following model to create a petition for your own cause.

Title of Petition

A petition from: *[name of group]*
Addressed to: *[name of lawmaker or agency]*
We the undersigned would like to bring to your attention the following matter, with these recommendations for legislative changes.

_____
_____
_____

Agreed upon by:

Name	Address	Telephone Number
1.		
2.		
3.		
4.		

It is important to be sure that everyone who signs your petition is eligible to vote in the area you are representing.

Name _____ Date _____

REVIEW
CHAPTER

3

Section 1

GUIDED READING *The Jeffersonian Era*

A. As you read about Jefferson's presidency, write answers to the questions below.

Key Trends in the Jeffersonian Era
1. How did Jefferson simplify the federal government?
2. How did the Federalists lose power during the Jefferson administration?
3. How did the election of 1800 change all presidential elections to come?

Key Events in the Jeffersonian Era
4. What was the long-term importance of the Supreme Court's decision in *Marbury* v. *Madison?*
5. How did the Louisiana Purchase affect the United States and its government?
6. What were the important results of the Lewis and Clark expedition?

B. On the back of this paper, explain how each of the following are related:

  war hawks   James Monroe   Monroe Doctrine

C. On the back of this paper, identify each of the following:

  Jeffersonian republicanism   John Marshall   Oregon Territory

Name _____   Date _____

GUIDED READING *The Age of Jackson*

A. As you read about the Jacksonian era, write answers to the questions about events
that appear on the time line.

1824	John Quincy Adams wins the presidency.	→	1. Why did the House of Representatives support John Quincy Adams over Andrew Jackson?
1830	Congress passes the Indian Removal Act. Jackson forces the Cherokee and Choctaw from their lands.	→	2. What did the Indian Removal Act call for?
1832	The nullification crisis comes to a head.	→	3. What was John C. Calhoun's theory of nullification?
1834	National Republicans form the Whig Party.	→	4. How did the style of politics change during the Age of Jackson?
1836	Martin Van Buren wins the presidency.		
1837	The Panic of 1837 bankrupts many businesses and causes deep unemployment.	→	5. How did Jackson's policies contribute to the Panic of 1837?

B. On the back of this paper, identify or explain each of the following:

Henry Clay   **Missouri Compromise**   **spoils system**

Name _____ Date _____

A. As you read about expansion to areas of the West, fill out the charts.

Despite the hardships of the journey and the difficult living conditions at journey's end, numbers of Americans migrated west during the mid-19th century.

	Texas	Oregon	Utah
1. Who went?			
2. Why did they go?			
3. How did they get there?			
4. What did they find when they got there?			

Discuss the causes and effects of the treaty to end the war with Mexico.

5. Treaty of Guadalupe Hidalgo
Causes:
Results:

B. On the back of this paper, briefly explain the relationship among the following:

Stephen F. Austin   **the Alamo**   **Sam Houston**

C. On the back of this paper, define the following:

manifest destiny   **Oregon Trail**   **Republic of California**

Name _____ Date _____

REVIEW CHAPTER
3
Section 4

GUIDED READING *The Market Revolution*

A. As you read about the formation of the national market economy, fill out the charts.

How did these innovations and inventions help expand the national market economy?	
1. Entrepreneurial activity	
2. Telegraph	
3. Steamboat	
4. Railroad	
5. Canals	
6. Steel plow	

How did these developments affect the lives of workers?	
7. Textile mills	
8. National Trades' Union	
9. *Commonwealth* v. *Hunt*	
10. Industrialization	

B. On the back of this paper, briefly explain how the people or innovations in each set are related:

1. **free enterprise   entrepreneurs   Samuel F. B. Morse**
2. **market revolution   Lowell textile mills   strike**

REVIEW
CHAPTER
3
Section 5

GUIDED READING *Reforming American Society*

A. As you read about reform movements, answer the questions below.

What ideas and practices did each of the following promote?
1. African-American church
2. *The Liberator*
3. Seneca Falls convention
4. Transcendentalism

5. What people and events shaped the abolition movement the most?
6. How did the African-American church interpret the message of Christianity?
7. How effective were efforts to reform education for women?

B. On the back of this paper, briefly describe the relationship of each of the following
to the reform movements of the 1880s.

William Lloyd Garrison	**Ralph Waldo Emerson**	**Elizabeth Cady Stanton**
Nat Turner	**Sojourner Truth**	**Frederick Douglass**

BUILDING VOCABULARY *The Growth of a Young Nation*

A. Matching Write the letter of the term or name on the line that best matches its description.

a. Trail of Tears
b. Henry Clay
c. Treaty of Guadalupe Hildago
d. Louisiana Purchase
e. abolition

f. John Calhoun
g. Nat Turner
h. impressment
i. Seneca Falls convention
j. Alamo

_____ 1. promoted the theory of nullification

_____ 2. site of famous Texas Revolution battle

_____ 3. British practice of seizing American sailors

_____ 4. agreement ending the Mexican-American War

_____ 5. Cherokee's journey of hardship and death to Indian Territory

_____ 6. early milestone in the fight for women's rights

_____ 7. roughly doubled the size of the United States

_____ 8. leader of well-known slave rebellion

_____ 9. movement to end slavery

_____ 10. promoter of the American System

B. Completion Select the term or name that best completes the sentence.

market revolution
judicial review
Nat Turner

manifest destiny
Frederick Douglass
James K. Polk

free enterprise
Missouri Compromise
Jeffersonian republicanism

1. _____ was a former slave who became a prominent abolitionist.

2. The period in U.S. history in which people bought and sold goods rather than make them for themselves.

3. _____ was a belief that prompted many Americans to begin settling the West.

4. By dividing the Louisiana Territory into slave and free states, the _____ temporarily quieted the debate over slavery.

5. _____ held that people should control the government and that a simple government was best.

C. Writing Write a paragraph describing the growing power of the national government using the following terms.

Marbury v. *Madison*   **John Marshall**   **judicial review**

                    James Monroe   **Monroe Doctrine**

CHAPTER 3

Section 1

SKILLBUILDER PRACTICE *Making Inferences*

Do you know the expression "to read between the lines"? It means to look for information that is implied rather than stated directly by the author or speaker. Reading between the lines requires you to look for clues that give you insights into what a person really believes or thinks. These insights are known as inferences. Practice making inferences by reading the quote on this page by Thomas Jefferson. Then answer the questions that follow. (See Skillbuilder Handbook, p. R10.)

"With all [our] blessings, what more is necessary to make us a happy and a prosperous people? Still one thing more, fellow citizens—a wise and frugal Government, which shall restrain men from injuring one another, shall leave them otherwise free to regulate their own pursuits of industry and improvement, and shall not take from the mouth of labor the bread that it has earned. This is the sum of good government."

from Thomas Jefferson's First Inaugural Address, 1801

1. What does Jefferson say are the goals of a good government?

_____

_____

_____

2. What can you infer from this list of goals about Jefferson's attitude toward government spending? Explain.

_____

_____

3. What can you infer about Jefferson's attitude toward taxation? Explain.

_____

_____

4. Based on this quotation, would you expect Jefferson to increase or decrease the power of the federal government during his term of office?

_____

5. What evidence on text page 113 supports your inference?

_____

_____

_____

Name _____ Date _____

SKILLBUILDER PRACTICE *Synthesizing*

The foreign policies of John Quincy Adams reflected a growing sense of national-
ism in the new United States. Read the definition of nationalism and the examples
given below, and tell how each example does or does not illustrate nationalism.
(See Skillbuilder Handbook, p. R19.)

Nationalism Nationalism is a philosophy that stresses national welfare
ahead of sectional or regional concerns. It also dictates that leaders give
top priority to national interests in foreign affairs.

Among the people of a country, nationalism means having a strong
feeling of being a part of the nation and sharing in the nation's culture
and heritage with the rest of the population. Nationalism often shows itself
in the people's patriotism, in their pride in the country and its heroes and
leaders, and in loyalty to what the nation stands for.

Example 1 From the War of 1812, the Battle of New Orleans became
a source of legends about American superiority. Over time, historians have
realized that the British probably lost that battle because their advancing
soldiers paused and became sitting ducks for American artillery. However,
immediately after the battle, the tale spread that Americans won the battle
because sharp-shooting frontiersmen from Kentucky were able to pick off
British troops with incredible accuracy. Americans were proud of the successes
of their militia over professional soldiers, and they chose to believe that the
victory of the Battle of New Orleans was a victory of amateurs.

Example 2 Between 1819 and 1821, Congress plunged into a lengthy
controversy over admitting Missouri to the Union as slave state. Noting
that every president since John Adams had been a Virginian, Federalists
portrayed the admission of Missouri as part of a conspiracy to perpetuate
the rule of Virginia slave holders. Republicans pointed out the sudden emergence
of a vocal anti-slavery block in the House of Representatives, which included
many northern Federalists. Some Republicans began to see efforts to restrict
slavery as part of a Federalist plot to gain political power by dividing northern
and southern Republicans. The issue of slavery had become woven into the
general distrust between the political parties and between sections of the country.

1. Example 1 **does** or **does not** (circle one) illustrate nationalism because

_____

_____

_____

2. Example 2 **does** or **does not** (circle one) illustrate nationalism because

_____

_____

_____

Name _____   Date _____

SKILLBUILDER PRACTICE *Analyzing Assumptions and Biases*

During the mid-1800s, a number of Americans supported expansion of the United States to all points of the continent. Read the following passage, then follow the directions below. (See Skillbuilder Handbook, p. R15.)

After Texas became a U.S. territory, expansionists continued to look for new areas to bring under the wing of the United States. One such area, the Yucatán peninsula of Mexico, was especially appealing because of its geographical location enclosing the southern part of the Gulf of Mexico. In fact, the white population of Yucatán begged the United States for help in their defense against the native peoples there. American newspaper editors with expansionist views wrote enthusiastically about the possibility of adding another star—representing Yucatán—to the nation's flag. An editorial in the New York *Herald* on May 12, 1848, expressed even more extreme views:

> Mexico now lies at the feet of the United States, fit for nothing but to be moulded and shaped in such form as we choose to give it. In such a new position of things, it may be well to ascertain whether it would not be more advis-

able to make arrangements for the absorption of all Mexico, including Yucatán . . . in some shape or form calculated to preserve the integrity of our institutions, as well as to give Mexico a chance to redeem her character and pretensions to [being] a civilized people. She is full of everything that is valuable; but the present race which possesses control seems to be utterly incapable of developing her resources. Annexed to the United States as a territory and possessing such a stable government as we could give her previous to her ultimate admission, the influence from this country would be great . . . in giving an entirely new character to her resources and population.

Fill out the chart below to help you analyze the assumptions underlying the newspaper editorial.

Assumption about the United States:

This assumption is **directly stated** or **implied.** (circle one) It is based on **evidence** or **bias.** (circle one)

Assumption about Mexico:

This assumption is **directly stated** or **implied.** (circle one) It is based on **evidence** or **bias.** (circle one)

SKILLBUILDER PRACTICE *Identifying Problems*

Women faced many problems in the early 1800s, not the least of which was getting the public to accept the need for change. Read the passage, then complete the chart below. First, list three problems faced by the women; then say whether the problem was stated directly or implied by people's actions; finally, list clues that helped you identify each problem. (See Skillbuilder Handbook, p. R5.)

The campaign for women's rights had less impact on the public than other reform issues did. The causes of temperance and school reform were much more popular, and abolitionism stirred up more people. Although they called for voting rights as early as 1848, women did not obtain the right to vote until 1920, 72 years later.

One reason for the slow progress toward women's rights was that small gains in a few places satisfied many women. For example, by the time of the Civil War, several states had given married women the right to own property. Women who otherwise might have worked for equal rights felt that progress had already been made and no more action was needed.

Another reason was the close association of women's rights to the abolition of slavery. In the first part of the 1800s, abolition was an unpopular movement in American society. Much of the general public scorned reform in both areas. Ironically, however, slavery was abolished 55 years before women were granted the right to vote.

The campaign for full equality for women also suffered as energy and attention were directed at temperance and educational reforms. Drunkenness contributed to a breakdown in family life and changes were needed in the ways children were educated in the country. Many women who might otherwise have worked on behalf of women's rights found that they could easily work for temperance and educational reforms and still be seen as taking care of their families, rather than as going against the popular ideal of women's place being in the home.

Problem	Directly stated or implied?	Clue words and phrases
1.		
2.		
3.		

RETEACHING ACTIVITY *The Jeffersonian Era*

Finding Main Ideas

The following questions deal with events of the Jeffersonian Era. Answer them in the space provided.

1. How did the election of 1800 lead to passage of the Twelfth Amendment?

_____

_____

2. What is the principle of judicial review?

_____

_____

3. What was significant about the Louisiana Purchase?

_____

_____

4. What were the consequences of the War of 1812?

_____

_____

5. What contributions did Secretary of State John Quincy Adams make to the nation's territorial expansion?

_____

_____

6. What did the Monroe Doctrine declare?

_____

_____

RETEACHING ACTIVITY *The Age of Jackson*

A. Reading Comprehension Write *T* in the blank if the statement is true. If the
statement is false, write *F* in the blank and then write the corrected statement on
the line below.

_____ 1. Industry first took hold in the South because agriculture there was not highly profitable and
many citizens were ready to embrace new forms of manufacturing.

_____

_____ 2. The emergence of cotton as a major crop in the South led to the need for more field laborers
and thus the growth of slavery.

_____

_____ 3. The American System consisted of establishing a protective tariff, abolishing the national bank,
and sponsoring internal improvements.

_____

_____ 4. Under the Missouri Compromise the Louisiana Territory was divided into two parts—one slave,
one free.

_____

B. Summarizing Andrew Jackson's beliefs and actions regarding the important
issues of his presidency in the chart shown here.

Nullification Crisis	National Bank	Indian Removal

REVIEW
CHAPTER
3
Section 3

RETEACHING ACTIVITY *Manifest Destiny*

A. Chronological Order Number the events of the nation's expansion in the order in which they occurred.

_____ 1. Mormons settle at the Great Salt Lake

_____ 2. American stake claim to the Republic of California.

_____ 3. Gadsden Purchase establishes current borders of U.S.

_____ 4. Battle of the Alamo

_____ 5. California's population exceeds 100,000

_____ 6. Texas joins the Union

_____ 7. Treaty of Guadalupe Hidalgo

_____ 8. Mexico wins independence from Spain

B. Reading Comprehension Choose the word that most accurately completes the sentences below.

War with Mexico	Horace Greeley	New Mexico
California	James Marshall	slavery
War for Texas Independence	land	Missouri

1. Disputes between the Mexican government and American settlers in Texas arose over the issue of

    _____.

2. "Remember the Alamo!" became a powerful rallying cry in the _____.

3. The man who uttered the famous phrase, "Go west, young man!" was _____.

4. The abundance of _____ was the greatest attraction to western settlers.

5. Under the Treaty of Guadalupe Hildago, Mexico ceded the territories _____ and _____.

REVIEW CHAPTER

3

Section 4

RETEACHING ACTIVITY *The Market Revolution*

Summarizing Choose the best answer for each item. Write the letter of your answer in the blank.

_____ 1. Samuel Morse invented the
   a. steam engine.
   b. steel plow.
   c. telegraph.
   d. cotton gin.

_____ 2. The groups that benefited the most from John Deere's invention was
   a. farmers.
   b. railroad operators.
   c. factory workers.
   d. artisans.

_____ 3. The employees of the Lowell textile mills were mostly
   a. men.
   b. women.
   c. enslaved African Americans.
   d. children.

_____ 4. Many Irish immigrants faced prejudice in America because of their
   a. skin color.
   b. political beliefs.
   c. language.
   d. religion.

_____ 5. The case of *Commonwealth* v. *Hunt* was a victory for
   a. banks.
   b. business owners.
   c. workers.
   d. Native Americans.

_____ 6. During the early 1800s, most Americans lived
   a. in rural areas.
   b. in cities.
   c. west of the Mississippi.
   d. near railroads.

Name _____ Date _____

RETEACHING ACTIVITY *Reforming American Society*

Summarizing Summarize the significant efforts of the abolition and women's movement in the chart below and then answer the question that follows.

```
                    ┌─────────────────────────┐
                    │    REFORM MOVEMENTS     │
                    └─────────────────────────┘
                         /              \
        ┌──────────────────────┐   ┌──────────────────────┐
        │      ABOLITION       │   │   WOMEN'S ISSUES     │
        │                      │   │                      │
        │                      │   │                      │
        │                      │   │                      │
        │                      │   │                      │
        │                      │   │                      │
        │                      │   │                      │
        └──────────────────────┘   └──────────────────────┘
```

Which movement do you think would face the most difficulties ahead? Why?

_____

_____

_____

GEOGRAPHY APPLICATION: REGION
Mexico Cedes Land to the United States

Section 3   *Directions: Read the paragraphs below and study the map carefully. Then answer the questions that follow.*

Long-standing tensions between the United States and Mexico erupted into warfare in 1846.

A year earlier the United States had angered Mexico by annexing the independent Republic of Texas and making it a state. Mexico and Texas were still in dispute over the exact borders of Texas, with Mexico refusing to concede that they extended down to the Rio Grande.

Then, when the United States sought to buy from Mexico the disputed Texas territory, as well as the territories of New Mexico and California, the Mexicans refused and war broke out.

The war with Mexico lasted until 1848. At its conclusion the two parties signed a treaty that ceded to the United States, for $15 million, all the territory it sought. Five years later, seeking a low-mountain passage through which to build a trans-continental railroad, the United States bought, for $10 million, a strip of land in a deal called the Gadsden Purchase. Thus, between 1845 and 1853 the United States gained more than a million square miles of land from Mexico.

The map below shows the states formed from the land and the years they achieved statehood.

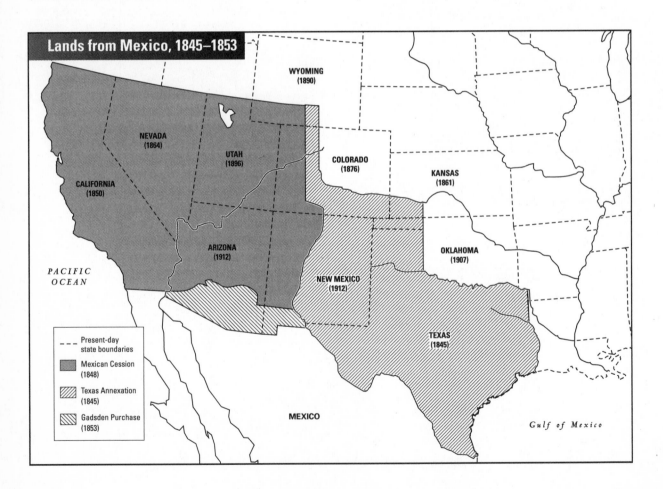

Interpreting Text and Visuals

1. How many present-day states are included, at least in part, in the acquisition from Mexico?

   _____

2. Look at the Mexican Cession and think about where the United States began back in 1776. What borders did the United States gain when it acquired this territory?

   _____

   _____

3. Which state acquired part of its land from the Mexican Cession, part from the Gadsden Purchase, and part from the Texas Annexation?

   _____

4. In what state is most of the land of the Gadsden Purchase found? _____

5. Which states were fashioned in their entirety from these territories? _____

   _____

6. How much did acquiring these three parcels of land cost the United States?

   _____

7. Statehood came early for some of the lands acquired from Mexico, such as California and Texas. For other lands, however, statehood came later and for some, not until the 20th century. What might account for the difference in the dates of statehood for these lands?

   _____

   _____

   _____

   _____

   _____

   _____

REVIEW CHAPTER

3

Section 2

OUTLINE MAP *The Indian Removal Act of 1830*

A. Review the map of the Indian Removal Act on textbook page 125. Then label the following bodies of water, areas of original Native American settlements, and territories on the accompanying outline map. In addition, label all the existing states. (Abbreviations for states are acceptable; if necessary, use the map on textbook pages A6–A7.)

Bodies of Water	**Native American Settlements**		**Territories**
Gulf of Mexico	Cherokee	Potawatomi	Unorganized Territory
Atlantic Ocean	Chickasaw	Miami	Indian Territory
Mississippi River	Creek	Shawnee and Seneca	Arkansas Territory (state, 1836)
Lake Michigan	Choctaw	Seminole	Florida Territory
Lake Erie			
Missouri River			
Ohio River			

B. After completing the map, use it to answer the following questions.

1. The routes of what two Native American groups crossed over part of the Gulf of Mexico?

   _____

2. "Down the Ohio, up the Mississippi and westward on the Missouri River" describes the principal route of which group? _____

3. In what present-day states was the Cherokee Nation once found?_____

   _____

4. How many principal routes did the Cherokee take to Indian Territory?_____

   Through which states and territory did the routes take the Cherokee? _____

   _____

5. How did the destination of the Potawatomi, Miami, Shawnee, and Seneca differ from that of the Cherokee, Chickasaw, Choctaw, Creek, and Seminole?_____

   _____

6. About how many miles long was the route traveled by the Seminoles? _____

Native American Movement, 1830–1842

N

| 0 | | 300 Miles |
| 0 | | 300 Kilometers |

40°N

30°N

90°W   80°W

PRIMARY SOURCE *from* The Hayne-Webster Debates

One of the most famous debates in Congress began on January 19, 1830. Robert Y. Hayne from South Carolina and Daniel Webster from Massachusetts debated issues such as public land policy, western expansion, and slavery. As you read these excerpts, think about the senators' positions on states' rights versus federal authority.

from Senator Hayne's Speech, January 21

Who, then, Mr. President, are the true friends of the Union? Those who would confine the federal government strictly within the limits prescribed by the constitution; who would preserve to the States and the people all powers not expressly delegated; who would make this a federal and not a national union, and who, administering the government in a spirit of equal justice, would make it a blessing and not a curse. And who are its enemies? Those who are in favor of consolidation—who are constantly stealing power from the States, and adding strength to the federal government. Who, assuming an unwarrantable jurisdiction over the States and the people, undertake to regulate the whole industry and capital of the country. But, sir, of all descriptions of men, I consider those as the worst enemies of the Union, who sacrifice the equal rights which belong to every member of the confederacy, to combinations of interested majorities, for personal or political objects. . . .

Sir, as to the doctrine that the federal government is the exclusive judge of the extent as well as the limitations of its powers, it seems to me to be utterly subversive of the sovereignty and independence of the States. It makes but little difference, in my estimation, whether Congress or the Supreme Court are invested with this power. If the federal government, in all, or any of its departments, are to prescribe the limits of its own authority, and the States are bound to submit to the decision, and are not to be allowed to examine and decide for themselves, when the barriers of the constitution shall be overleaped, this is practically "a government without limitation of powers."

The States are at once reduced to mere petty corporations, and the people are entirely at your mercy. I have but one more word to add. In all the efforts that have been made by South Carolina to resist the unconstitutional laws which Congress has extended over them, she has kept steadily in view the preservation of the Union, by the only means

by which she believes it can be long preserved—a firm, manly, and steady resistance against usurpation. The measures of the federal government have, it is true, prostrated her interests, and will soon involve the whole South in irretrievable ruin. But even this evil, great as it is, is not the chief ground of our complaints. It is the principle involved in the contest—a principle, which substituting the discretion of Congress for the limitations of the constitution, brings the States and the people to the feet of the federal government, and leaves them nothing they can call their own.

from Senator Webster's Reply, January 26–27

The proposition that, in case of a supposed violation of the Constitution by Congress, the states have a constitutional right to interfere and annul the law of Congress is the proposition of the gentleman [Hayne]. I do not admit it. If the gentleman had intended no more than to assert the right of revolution for justifiable cause, he would have said only what all agree to. But I cannot conceive that there can be a middle course, between submission to the laws, when regularly pronounced constitutional, on the one hand, and open resistance, which is revolution or rebellion, on the other.

I say, the right of a state to annul a law of Congress cannot be maintained but on the ground of the inalienable right of man to resist oppression; that is to say, upon the ground of revolution. I admit that there is an ultimate violent remedy, above the Constitution and in defiance of the Constitution, which may be resorted to when a revolution is to be justified. But I do not admit that, under the Constitution and in conformity with it, there is any mode in which a state government, as a member of the Union, can interfere and stop the progress of the general government, by force of her own laws, under any circumstances whatever. . . .

Mr. President, I have thus stated the reasons of my dissent to the doctrines which have been advanced and maintained. I am conscious of having detained you and the Senate much too long. I was drawn into the debate with no previous deliberation, such as is suited to the discussion of so grave and important a subject. But it is a subject of which my heart is full, and I have not been willing to suppress the utterance of its spontaneous sentiments. I cannot, even now, persuade myself to relinquish it without expressing once more my deep conviction that, since it respects nothing less than the Union of the States, it is of most vital and essential importance to the public happiness.

I profess, sir, in my career hitherto, to have kept steadily in view the prosperity and honor of the whole country, and the preservation of our federal Union. It is to that Union we owe our safety at home, and our consideration and dignity abroad. It is to that Union that we are chiefly indebted for whatever makes us most proud of our country— that Union we reached only by the discipline of our virtues in the severe school of adversity. It had its origin in the necessities of disordered finance, prostrate commerce, and ruined credit. Under its benign influences, these great interests immediately awoke, as from the dead, and sprang forth with newness of life. Every year of its duration has teemed with fresh proofs of its utility and its blessings. And although our territory has stretched out wider and wider, and our population spread farther and farther, they have not outrun its protection or its benefits. It has been to us all a copious fountain of national, social, and personal happiness.

I have not allowed myself, sir, to look beyond the Union, to see what might lie hidden in the dark recess behind. I have not coolly weighed the chances of preserving liberty when the bonds that unite us together shall be broken asunder. I have not accustomed myself to hang over the precipice of disunion, to see whether, with my short sight, I can fathom the depth of the abyss below; nor could I regard him as a safe counselor in the affairs in this government whose thoughts should be mainly bent on considering, not how the Union may best be preserved but how tolerable might be the condi-

tion of the people when it should be broken up and destroyed. While the Union lasts, we have high, exciting, gratifying prospects spread out before us, for us and our children. Beyond that I seek not to penetrate the veil.

God grant that in my day, at least, that curtain may not rise! God grant that on my vision never may be opened what lies behind! When my eyes shall be turned to behold for the last time the sun in heaven, may I not see him shining on the broken and dishonored fragments of a once glorious Union; on states dissevered, discordant, belligerent; on a land rent with civil feuds, or drenched, it may be, in fraternal blood! Let their last feeble and lingering glance rather behold the gorgeous ensign of the republic, now known and honored throughout the earth, still full high advanced, its arms and trophies streaming in their original luster, not a stripe erased or polluted, not a single star obscured, bearing for its motto, no such miserable interrogatory as "What is all this worth?" nor those other words of delusion and folly, "Liberty first and Union afterwards"; but everywhere spread all over in characters of living light, blazing on all its ample folds, as they float over the sea and over the land, and in every wind under the whole heavens, that other sentiment, dear to every true American heart— Liberty and Union, now and forever, one and inseparable!

from Orations of American Orators in The World's Great Classics, II (New York, 1900) and *The Writings and Speeches of Daniel Webster*, Vol. VI, (Boston: 1903).

Activity Options

1. Work with a partner to make a Venn diagram in which you compare and contrast the senators' positions on the authority of the federal government. Then share your diagrams with the class.
2. Deliver one of these speech excerpts—Hayne's or Webster's—to the class. Then discuss with your classmates which excerpt you think is most effective and why.

REVIEW CHAPTER 3

Section 3

PRIMARY SOURCE *from* James K. Polk's Speech on War with Mexico

President James K. Polk and his cabinet agreed to send the following war message to Congress before word of a Mexican attack on American soldiers at Matamoras had reached Washington. As you read this excerpt from Polk's message, think about why he supports a war with Mexico.

The strong desire to establish peace with Mexico on liberal and honorable terms, and the readiness of this Government to regulate and adjust our boundary and other causes of difference with that power on such fair and equitable principles as would lead to permanent relations of the most friendly nature, induced me in September last [1845] to seek the reopening of diplomatic relations between the two countries. Every measure adopted on our part had for its object the furtherance of these desired results. In communicating to Congress a succinct statement of the injuries which we had suffered from Mexico, and which have been accumulating during a period of more than twenty years, every expression that could tend to inflame the people of Mexico or defeat or delay a pacific result was carefully avoided. An envoy of the United States [John Slidell] repaired to Mexico with full powers, and bearing evidence of the most friendly dispositions, his mission has been unavailing. The Mexican Government not only refused to receive him or listen to his propositions, but after a long-continued series of menaces have at last invaded our territory and shed the blood of our fellow-citizens on our own soil. . . .

The grievous wrongs perpetrated by Mexico upon our citizens throughout a long period of years remain unredressed, and solemn treaties pledging her public faith for this redress have been disregarded. A government either unable or unwilling to enforce the execution of such treaties fails to perform one of its plainest duties.

Our commerce with Mexico has been almost annihilated. It was formerly highly beneficial to both nations, but our merchants have been deterred from prosecuting it by the system of outrage and extortion which the Mexican authorities have pursued against them, whilst their appeals through their own Government for indemnity have been made in vain. Our forbearance has gone to such an extreme as to be mistaken in its character. Had we acted with vigor in repelling the insults and redressing the injuries inflicted by Mexico at the commencement, we should doubtless have escaped all the difficulties in which we are now involved.

Instead of this, however, we have been exerting our best efforts to propitiate her good will. Upon the pretext that Texas, a nation as independent as herself, thought proper to unite its destinies with our own she has affected to believe that we have severed her rightful territory, and in official proclamation and manifestoes has repeatedly threatened to make war upon us for the purpose of reconquering Texas. In the meantime we have tried every effort at reconciliation. The cup of forbearance had been exhausted even before the recent information from the frontier of the Del Norte [Rio Grande]. But now, after reiterated menaces, Mexico has passed the boundary of the United States, has invaded our territory and shed American blood upon the American soil. She has proclaimed that hostilities have commenced, and that the two nations are now at war.

As war exists, and, notwithstanding all our efforts to avoid it, exists by the act of Mexico herself, we are called upon by every consideration of duty and patriotism to vindicate with decision the honor, the rights, and the interests of our country.

from *Opposing Viewpoints in American History*, vol. 1, *From Colonial Times to Reconstruction* (San Diego: Greenhaven Press, Inc.), 217–220.

Discussion Questions

1. What reasons for war did Polk cite in his message?
2. According to Polk, what steps had the United States taken to avoid war with Mexico?
3. Why do you think that Polk's message convinced Congress to vote to go to war with Mexico?

Name _____ Date _____

PRIMARY SOURCE Propaganda Images

REVIEW CHAPTER **3**
Section 5

Proslavery advocates used the Bible to defend slavery and promoted the idea that enslaved Africans had an improved standard of living. To find out how proslavery advocates illustrated the benefits of slavery, study the following before-and-after pictures from a proslavery pamphlet entitled Bible Defense of Slavery.

THE NEGRO IN HIS OWN COUNTRY.

THE NEGRO IN AMERICA.

Courtesy of the Chicago Historical Society

Discussion Questions

1. According to the "before" picture, what were the drawbacks of living in Africa?
2. What were the benefits of slavery according to the "after" picture?

3. What before-and-after images do you think a 19th-century abolitionist could have used to counteract the arguments of proslavery advocates and to illustrate the horrors of slavery?

Name _____ Date _____

REVIEW CHAPTER

3

Section 5

PRIMARY SOURCE *from* The Seneca Falls "Declaration of Sentiments"

At the first women's rights convention, Elizabeth Cady Stanton and Lucretia Mott issued this statement modeled on the Declaration of Independence. What grievances did the women express in this portion of their Declaration?

When, in the course of human events, it becomes necessary for one portion of the family of man to assume among the people of the earth a position different from that which they have hitherto occupied, but one to which the laws of nature and of nature's God entitle them, a decent respect to the opinions of mankind requires that they should declare the causes that impel them to such a course.

We hold these truths to be self-evident: that all men and women are created equal; that they are endowed by their Creator with certain inalienable rights; that among these are life, liberty, and the pursuit of happiness. . . .

The history of mankind is a history of repeated injuries and usurpations on the part of man toward woman, having in direct object the establishment of an absolute tyranny over her. To prove this, let facts be submitted to a candid world.

He has never permitted her to exercise her inalienable right to the elective franchise.

He has compelled her to submit to laws, in the formation of which she had no voice.

He has withheld from her rights which are given to the most ignorant and degraded men—both natives and foreigners.

Having deprived her of this first right of a citizen, the elective franchise, thereby leaving her without representation in the halls of legislation, he has oppressed her on all sides.

He has made her, if married, in the eye of the law, civilly dead.

He has taken away from her all right in property, even to the wages she earns.

He has made her, morally, an irresponsible being, as she can commit many crimes with impunity, provided they be done in the presence of her husband. In the covenant of marriage, she is compelled to promise obedience to her husband, he becoming to all intents and purposes, her master—the law giving him power to deprive her of her liberty, and to administer chastisement.

He has so framed the laws of divorce, as to what shall be the proper causes, and in case of separation, to whom the guardianship of the children shall be given, as to be wholly regardless of the happiness of women—the law, in all cases, going upon a false supposition of the supremacy of man, and giving all power into his hands.

After depriving her of all rights as a married woman, if single, and the owner of property, has taxed her to support a government which recognizes her only when her property can be made profitable to it.

He has monopolized nearly all the profitable employments, and from those she is permitted to follow, she receives but a scanty remuneration. He closes against her all the avenues to wealth and distinction which he considers most honorable to himself. As a teacher of theology, medicine, or law, she is not known.

He has denied her the facilities for obtaining a thorough education, all colleges being closed against her. . . .

He has endeavored, in every way that he could, to destroy her confidence in her own powers, to lessen her self-respect and to make her willing to lead a dependent and abject life.

Now, in view of this entire disenfranchisement of one-half the people of this country, their social and religious degradation—in view of the unjust laws above mentioned, and because women do feel themselves aggrieved, oppressed, and fraudulently deprived of their most sacred rights, we insist that they have immediate admission to all the rights and privileges which belong to them as citizens of the United States. . . .

from Elizabeth Cady Stanton, Susan B. Anthony, and Matilda Joslyn Gage, eds., *History of Woman Suffrage*, vol. 1 (1881).

Activity Options

1. Working with a partner, analyze the declaration and list the rights women have gained since 1848.
2. Write a paragraph in which you compare the purpose and language of the "Declaration of Sentiments" and the Declaration of Independence.

REVIEW CHAPTER 3

Section 3

LITERATURE SELECTION *from* **Roughing It**

by Mark Twain

Like other Americans who were lured by the promise of the western frontier, Mark Twain traveled to the Nevada Territory in 1861. He bought mining stock, entered timber claims, and prospected for silver. As you read this excerpt from Twain's travel book Roughing It *(1872), think about the ups and downs of his get-rich-quick scheme.*

Chapter XXVI

By and by I was smitten with the silver fever. "Prospecting parties" were leaving for the mountains every day, and discovering and taking possession of rich silver-bearing lodes and ledges of quartz. Plainly this was the road to fortune. The great "Gould and Curry" mine was held at three or four hundred dollars a foot when we arrived; but in two months it had sprung up to eight hundred. The "Ophir" had been worth only a mere trifle, a year gone by, and now it was selling at nearly *four thousand dollars a foot!* Not a mine could be named that had not experienced an astonishing advance in value within a short time. Everybody was talking about these marvels. Go where you would, you heard nothing else, from morning till far into the night. Tom So-and-So had sold out of the "Amanda Smith" for $40,000—hadn't a cent when he "took up" the ledge six months ago. John Jones had sold half his interest in the "Bald Eagle and Mary Ann" for $65,000, gold coin, and gone to the States for his family. The widow Brewster "struck it rich" in the "Golden Fleece" and sold ten feet for $18,000—hadn't money enough to buy a crape bonnet when Sing-Sing Tommy killed her husband at Baldy Johnson's wake last spring. . . .

I would have been more or less than human if I had not gone mad like the rest. Cart-loads of solid silver bricks, as large as pigs of lead, were arriving from the mills every day, and such sights as that gave substance to the wild talk about me. I succumbed and grew frenzied as the craziest.

Every few days news would come of the discovery of a brand-new mining region; immediately the papers would teem with accounts of its richness, and away the surplus population would scamper to take possession. By the time I was fairly inoculated with the disease, "Esmeralda" had just run and "Humboldt" was beginning to shriek for attention. "Humboldt! Humboldt!" was the new cry, and straightway Humboldt, the newest of the new, the richest of the rich, the most marvellous of the marvellous discoveries in silver-land, was occupying two columns of the public prints to "Esmeralda's" one. I was just on the point of starting to Esmeralda, but turned with the tide and got ready for Humboldt. . . .

Chapter XXVIII

After leaving the Sink [river basin], we traveled along the Humboldt river a little way. People accustomed to the monster mile-wide Mississippi, grow accustomed to associating the term "river" with a high degree of watery grandeur. Consequently, such people feel rather disappointed when they stand on the shores of the Humboldt or the Carson and find that a "river" in Nevada is a sickly rivulet which is just the counterpart of the Erie canal in all respects save that the canal is twice as long and four times as deep. One of the pleasantest and most invigorating exercises one can contrive is to run and jump across the Humboldt river till he is overheated, and then drink it dry.

On the fifteenth day we completed our march of two hundred miles and entered Unionville, Humboldt county, in the midst of a driving snow-storm. Unionville consisted of eleven cabins and a liberty-pole. Six of the cabins were strung along one side of a deep canyon, and the other five faced them. The rest of the landscape was made up of bleak mountain walls that rose so high into the sky from both sides of the canyon that the village was left, as it were, far down in the bottom of a crevice. It was always daylight on the mountain tops a long time before the darkness lifted and revealed Unionville.

> *Cart-loads of solid silver bricks, as large as pigs of lead, were arriving from the mills every day.*

We built a small, rude cabin in the side of the crevice and roofed it with canvas, leaving a corner open to serve as a chimney, through which the cattle used to tumble occasionally, at night, and mash our furniture and interrupt our sleep. It was very cold weather and fuel was scarce. Indians brought brush and bushes several miles on their backs; and when we could catch a laden Indian it was well—and when we could not (which was the rule, not the exception), we shivered and bore it.

I confess, without shame, that I expected to find masses of silver lying all about the ground. I expected to see it glittering in the sun on the mountain summits. I said nothing about this, for some instinct told me that I might possibly have an exaggerated idea about it, and so if I betrayed my thought I might bring derision upon myself. Yet I was as perfectly satisfied in my own mind as I could be of anything, that I was going to gather up, in a day or two, or at furthest a week or two, silver enough to make me satisfactorily wealthy—and so my fancy was already busy with plans for spending this money. The first opportunity that offered, I sauntered carelessly away from the cabin, keeping an eye on the other boys, and stopping and contemplating the sky when they seemed to be observing me; but as soon as the coast was manifestly clear, I fled away as guiltily as a thief might have done and never halted till I was far beyond sight and call. Then I began my search with a feverish excitement that was brimful of expectation—almost of certainty. I crawled about the ground, seizing and examining bits of stone, blowing the dust from them or rubbing them on my clothes, and then peering at them with anxious hope. Presently I found a bright fragment and my heart bounded! I hid behind a boulder and polished it and scrutinized it with a nervous eagerness and a delight that was more pronounced than absolute certainty itself could have afforded. The more I examined the fragment the more I was convinced that I had found the door to fortune. I marked the spot and carried away my specimen. Up and down the rugged mountain side I searched, with always increasing interest and always augmenting gratitude that I had come to Humboldt and come in time. Of all the experiences

I confess, without shame, that I expected to find masses of silver lying all about the ground. I expected to see it glittering in the sun on the mountain summits.

of my life, this secret search among the hidden treasures of silver-land was the nearest to unmarred ecstasy. It was a delirious revel. By and by, in the bed of a shallow rivulet, I found a deposit of shining yellow scales, and my breath almost forsook me! A gold mine, and in my simplicity I had been content with vulgar silver! I was so excited that I half believed my overwrought imagination was deceiving me. Then a fear came upon me that people might be observing me and would guess my secret. Moved by this thought, I made a circuit of the place, and ascended a knoll to reconnoiter. Solitude. No creature was near. Then I returned to my mine, fortifying myself against possible disappointment, but my fears were groundless—the shining scales were still there. I set about scooping them out, and for an hour I toiled down the windings of the stream and robbed its bed. But at last the descending sun warned me to give up the quest, and I turned homeward laden with wealth. As I walked along I could not help smiling at the thought of my being so excited over my fragment of silver when a nobler metal was almost under my nose. In this little time the former had so fallen in my estimation that once or twice I was on the point of throwing it away.

The boys were as hungry as usual, but I could eat nothing. Neither could I talk. I was full of dreams and far away. Their conversation interrupted the flow of my fancy somewhat, and annoyed me a little, too. I despised the sordid and commonplace things they talked about. But as they proceeded, it began to amuse me. It grew to be rare fun to hear them planning their poor little economies and sighing over possible privations and distresses when a gold mine, all our own, lay within sight of the cabin and I could point it out at any moment. Smothered hilarity began to oppress me, presently. It was hard to resist the impulse to burst out with exultation and reveal everything; but I did resist. I said within myself that I would filter the great news through my lips calmly and be serene as a summer morning while I watched its effect in their faces. I said:

"Where have you all been?"

"Prospecting."

"What did you find?"

"Nothing."

"Nothing? What do you think of the country?"

"Can't tell, yet," said Mr. Ballou, who was an old gold miner, and had likewise had considerable experience among the silver mines.

"Well, haven't you formed any sort of opinion?"

"Yes, a sort of a one. It's fair enough here, may be, but overrated. Seven thousand dollar ledges are scarce, though. That Sheba may be rich enough, but we don't own it; and besides, the rock is so full of base metals that all the science in the world can't work it. We'll not starve, here, but we'll not get rich, I'm afraid."

"So you think the prospect is pretty poor?"

"No name for it!"

"Well, we'd better go back, hadn't we?"

"Oh, not yet—of course not. We'll try it a riffle, first."

"Suppose, now—this is merely a supposition, you know—suppose you could find a ledge that would yield, say, a hundred and fifty dollars a ton— would that satisfy you?"

"Try us once!" from the whole party.

"Or suppose—merely a supposition, of course— suppose you were to find a ledge that would yield two thousand dollars a ton—would that satisfy you?"

"Here—what do you mean? What are you coming at? Is there some mystery behind all this?"

"Never mind. I am not saying anything. You know perfectly well there are no rich mines here— of course you do. Because you have been around and examined for yourselves. Anybody would know that, that had been around. But just for the sake of argument, suppose—in a kind of general way— suppose some person were to tell you that two-thousand-dollar ledges were simply contemptible— contemptible, understand—and that right yonder in sight of this very cabin there were piles of pure gold and pure silver—oceans of it—enough to make you all rich in twenty-four hours! Come!"

"I should say he was as crazy as a loon!" said old Ballou, but wild with excitement, nevertheless.

"Gentlemen," said I, "I don't know anything—I haven't been around, you know, and of course don't know anything—but all I ask of you is to cast your eye on *that*, for instance, and tell me what you think of it!" and I tossed my treasure before them.

> *"Suppose you could find a ledge that would yield, say, a hundred and fifty dollars a ton— would that satisfy you?"*

There was an eager scramble for it, and a closing of heads together over it under the candle-light. Then old Ballou said:

"Think of it? I think it is nothing but a lot of granite rubbish and nasty glittering mica that isn't worth ten cents an acre!"

So vanished my dream. So melted my wealth away. So toppled my airy castle to the earth and left me stricken and forlorn.

Moralizing, I observed, then, that "all that glitters is not gold."

Mr. Ballou said I could go further than that, and lay it up among my treasures of knowledge, that *nothing* that glitters is gold. So I learned then, once for all, that gold in its native state is but dull, unornamental stuff, and that only low-born metals excite the admiration of the ignorant with an ostentatious glitter. However, like the rest of the world, I still go on underrating men of gold and glorifying men of mica. Commonplace human nature cannot rise above that.

Research Options

1. With a small group of classmates, research how 19th-century prospectors like Mark Twain mined gold and silver. What tools did they use? What different techniques were used to mine gold or silver? (Refer to pages 212–213 in your textbook.) Plan and present a short demonstration for the class.

2. Find out more about 19th-century mining booms that lured pioneers to the West, including the California gold rush and the discovery of the Comstock Lode in Nevada. Then make a cause-and-effect diagram illustrating the effects of mining booms. Share your diagram with classmates.

3. Bret Harte wrote about the California gold rush and Jack London wrote about the Alaskan gold rush in the late 1800s. Find and read a story by either Harte or London. Then write a comparison-and-contrast essay to compare Twain's account with one of their stories.

REVIEW CHAPTER 3

Section 1

AMERICAN LIVES Tecumseh

Native American Nationalist

"The only way to stop this evil is for all the red men to unite in claiming a common and equal right in the land, as it was at first, and should be now—for it never was divided, but belongs to all."—Tecumseh, to William Henry Harrison (1810)

Tecumseh was a bold leader with great vision and compassion. But his dream of creating a Native American nation failed—in part because of his brother's impulsiveness and in part because of the failure of the Bristish to come to his aid.

Tecumseh (c. 1768–1813) was born near present-day Springfield, Ohio, the son of a Shawnee chief. When Tecumseh was not yet ten, his father failed to return home one day. Tecumseh found him dying, having been shot by whites. The event caused lifelong anger toward whites. When he was about 15, though, he was outraged to see some Shawnee burn a white settler at the stake. He thereafter treated his enemies humanely, and on occasion his force of will prevented atrocities.

He became a skilled warrior, fighting bravely at the Battle of Fallen Timbers. When various chiefs ceded much of Ohio, Tecumseh refused to sign the treaty. In the uneasy peace that followed, Tecumseh befriended a white woman, Rebecca Galloway. Learning to read English from her, he studied ancient and European history.

As whites continued to enter the Northwest, many tribes became weakened by disease and alcohol. One of those afflicted by drinking was Tecumseh's brother. In 1805, however, he suddenly stopped drinking, changed his name to Tenskwatawa—"The Prophet"—and began to preach. He and Tecumseh gathered followers.

From a base in Indiana, Tecumseh traveled across the country rallying Native Americans to his cause: to unite all Native American tribes into one nation powerful enough to resist the advances of white settlers. He spoke eloquently. An American general said, "I have heard many great orators, but I never saw one with the vocal powers of Tecumseh."

In August 1810, Tecumseh and The Prophet met with General William Henry Harrison, governor of Indiana Territory. Harrison wanted to buy more land. Tecumseh spoke of the folly of selling land and of the past mistreatment of the Native Americans. Next day, he demonstrated his point.

He sat on a log bench and invited Harrison to join him. As they talked, he moved along the bench, pushing Harrison until he fell off. When the general protested, Tecumseh replied that this was how the Native Americans were treated.

Tecumseh left the meeting to go south for more support. He warned The Prophet to avoid combat because the alliance was not yet ready. Harrison, meanwhile, was determined to attack the camp at Tippecanoe now that Tecumseh was absent. The Prophet yielded to the demands of some warriors and launched a surprise attack. Though losses were about even on both sides, the Native Americans abandoned their village. Harrison burned it to the ground and declared a great victory. Tecumseh was angry when he returned.

Tecumseh sought the help of the British. He fought valiantly in the War of 1812, joining in the capture of Fort Detroit. When the Americans won the Battle of Lake Erie, the British decided to abandon Detroit. Tecumseh felt betrayed. He compared the British to "the fat animal, that carries its tail upon its back, but when affrighted, he drops it between his legs and runs off." He forced the British to take a stand at the Battle of the Thames in 1813, organizing both Indian and British troops in defense. The British lines broke at the American attack, but Tecumseh's Native Americans held and fought fiercely until overwhelming numbers defeated them and Tecumseh was killed.

Questions

1. What do you think Tecumseh may have learned from studying European history?
2. Was Tecumseh's plan a good idea for Native Americans?
3. Could Tecumseh have prevented the battle at Tippecanoe? Explain.

AMERICAN LIVES Henry Clay

Westerner with a National Vision

*"I know no South, no North, no East, no West, to which I owe any allegiance. . . .
My allegiance is to the American Union."—Henry Clay, Senate speech (1850)*

From 1810 to 1850, Henry Clay helped shape national policy. He pushed for a government role in building the American economy. He also fashioned compromises to resolve the growing differences between North and South.

Clay (1777–1852) had only a few years of formal schooling, but soon went to work as a clerk in a Virginia court. He studied law and, once admitted to the bar, moved to frontier Kentucky where he achieved fame and power.

Clay was elected to the U.S. Senate in 1806 and then the House in 1810, where he won election as Speaker. Though young, he was a leader. Writing of him, a colleague said, "He stalks among men with an unanswerable and never doubting air of command." Angry at the British and Native American threat in the West, he urged war on Great Britain. He remained optimistic about the war even in the face of early defeats. President Madison named him one of the peace negotiators, and Clay's tough stand ensured that the United States did not give up its claim for the right to travel and trade on the Mississippi River.

During the 1810s, Clay played an increasingly major role in national politics. He made an enemy when he denounced Andrew Jackson's invasion of Spanish Florida. He made friends in Latin America, saying that the United States should recognize the new governments that had won independence from Spain. In 1820, he won House passage of the Missouri Compromise, resolving a crisis over slavery in the territories and earning the nickname "Great Pacifier."

Clay urged a wide-ranging program to promote American industry and commerce. He backed tariffs on imports to allow industry to grow. He called for new roads and canals to transport goods. These actions were required to establish American economic independence. "We are," he said "independent colonies of England—politically free, [but] commercially slaves."

Clay finished last among four candidates in the 1824 presidential election. With no candidate win-

ning the electoral vote, the election was thrown to the House. Clay gave his support to John Quincy Adams, earning the additional nickname of "President Maker." When Adams named him secretary of state, supporters of Andrew Jackson charged that a "corrupt bargain" had sold the presidency. One Jackson backer went so far as to call Clay "this being, so brilliant yet so corrupt, which, like a rotten mackerel by moonlight, shined and stunk." Clay challenged him to a duel, and both were wounded. Taking the appointment was a political mistake, and Clay was hounded by the charge for the rest of his life. He never won the presidency, an office he deeply desired.

He remained, however, a powerful figure in Washington, and worked on two more occasions to prevent sectional conflict. In 1833, South Carolina threatened to leave the Union over the tariff, which many in the South felt was too high. Clay helped calm the crisis by working out a compromise that gradually lowered the tariff.

His final compromise came in 1850, when conflict over slavery in the territories again threatened to dissolve the Union. A 73-year-old Clay proposed a package of bills, offering some favoring the North and others appealing to the South. Pleading with the Senate to pass the package, Clay made his last great speech: "I believe from the bottom of my soul that his measure is the re-union of this Union. I believe it is the dove of peace." Eventually, the bills were approved, and the sectional conflict that Clay dreaded was postponed—for a time. Two years later, he died. His body lay in state in the Capitol Rotunda for a day—the first person so honored.

Questions

1. Why did Kentucky offer more opportunities to Clay than Virginia might have?
2. How did Clay's economic and political plans both express his idea of nationalism?
3. How was Clay, from Kentucky, well suited to forge a North/South compromise?

GUIDED READING *The Divisive Politics of Slavery*

A. As you read about the events and decisions that led to the South's secession, fill out
the chart below.

	Supporters	Reasons for Their Support
1. Compromise of 1850	❏ Proslavery forces ❏ Antislavery forces	
2. Fugitive Slave Act	❏ Proslavery forces ❏ Antislavery forces	
3. Underground Railroad	❏ Proslavery forces ❏ Antislavery forces	
4. Kansas-Nebraska Act	❏ Proslavery forces ❏ Antislavery forces	
5. Republican Party	❏ Proslavery forces ❏ Antislavery forces	
6. *Dred Scott* decision	❏ Proslavery forces ❏ Antislavery forces	
7. The raid on Harpers Ferry	❏ Proslavery forces ❏ Antislavery forces	
8. The election of Lincoln to the presidency	❏ Proslavery forces ❏ Antislavery forces	

B. On the back of this paper, note something important that you learned about the
following:

Harriet Beecher Stowe   **Lincoln-Douglas debates**   **Jefferson Davis**

REVIEW CHAPTER
4
Section 2

GUIDED READING *The Civil War Begins*

A. As you read about the first years of the Civil War, briefly note the causes or effects (depending on which is missing) of each situation.

Causes	Effects
1. Confederate soldiers fire on Union troops in Fort Sumter. →	
2. →	Lincoln issues the Emancipation Proclamation.
3. The Union accepts African Americans as soldiers. →	
4. The Confederacy faces a food shortage due to the drain of manpower into the army. →	

B. On the back of this paper, write what you think is important about the following:

Bull Run   **Antietam**   **Robert E. Lee**

Name _____ Date _____

GUIDED READING *The North Takes Charge*

As you read about the final years of the Civil War and its consequences, make notes to answer the questions.

1863	Gettysburg →	1. Why is the battle of Gettysburg considered a turning point in the war?
	Gettysburg Address →	2. What did the Gettysburg Address help Americans to realize?
1864	Grant appointed commander of all Union armies →	3. What was Grant's overall strategy for defeating Lee's army? What tactics did he use?
	Sherman's march from Atlanta to the sea →	4. What was Sherman's goal in his march to the sea? What tactics did he use to accomplish that goal?
	Lincoln reelected	
1865	John Wilkes Booth →	5. After the war ended, why didn't Lincoln implement his plans for reunifying the nation?
	Impact of the war →	6. What were some of the political and economic changes brought about by the war?
	Thirteenth Amendment ratified →	7. What was the purpose of the Thirteenth Amendment?

GUIDED READING *Reconstruction and Its Effects*

A. As you read this section, make notes that summarize the changes that took place as
a result of Reconstruction. List the postwar problems, classifying each problem as
political, economic, or social. Then indicate how individuals and the government
responded to each difficulty or crisis.

Problems	Responses
1. Primarily political	
2. Primarily economic	
3. Primarily social	

B. On the back of this paper, identify or explain each of the following:

    Fifteenth Amendment   **scalawag**   **carpetbagger**   **sharecropping**   **Rutherford B. Hayes**

Name _____ Date _____

BUILDING VOCABULARY *The Union in Peril*

A. Completion Select the term or name that best completes the sentence.

carpetbagger	Antietam	Underground Railroad
Fort Sumter	scalawag	Radicals
Gettysburg	conscription	popular sovereignty

1. The Civil War got underway with the Confederate attack on _____.

2. The Reconstruction Act was the product of the _____, who wanted to punish the South and destroy the power of former slaveholders.

3. One of the most famous conductors on the _____, Harriet Tubman helped lead many slaves to freedom.

4. The tide of the war turned in the North's favor at the Battle of _____.

5. One group that rose to power during Reconstruction were the _____s, white Southerners who joined the Republican Party.

6. As the war dragged on, each side resorted to _____, a draft that forced men to serve in the army.

B. Matching Match the definition in the second column with the term or name in the first column. Write the appropriate letter next to the word.

_____ 1. Clara Barton   a. led destructive march through Georgia

_____ 2. Confederacy   b. Confederate military leader

_____ 3. William T. Sherman   c. Northerner in the post-war South

_____ 4. Freedmen's Bureau   d. President Lincoln's assassin

_____ 5. Harriet Beecher Stowe e. slave who sued for his freedom

_____ 6. Robert E. Lee   f. famous Union nurse

_____ 7. Appomattox Court House g. author of *Uncle Tom's Cabin*

_____ 8. carpetbagger   h. collective name of the secessionist states

_____ 9. John Wilkes Booth   i. site of the South's surrender

_____ 10. Dred Scott   j. provided services in the post-war South

C. Writing Write a paragraph about the dramatic changes that took place for African Americans during the Civil War era and Reconstruction using the following terms.

Emancipation Proclamation   Thirteenth Amendment   Fourteenth Amendment

Fifteenth Amendment   Ku Klux Klan

SKILLBUILDER PRACTICE *Creating Databases*

The years leading up to the Civil War were known for, among other things, a number of significant measures by the federal government. Creating a computer database of such information can help you to organize the data in a format that is both easy to retrieve and to examine. To gain more practice in creating databases, review Chapter 4; Section 1 and then complete the database shown here by filling in the missing information. (See Skillbuilder Handbook, p. R33.)

Significant Pre-Civil War Era Measures		
Measure	Year	Significance

Answer the following questions about other possible databases.

1. What categories might you use to create a database of Pre-Civil-War leaders?

_____

_____

2. What categories might you use to create a database of Pre-Civil-War political parties?

_____

_____

REVIEW CHAPTER 4
Section 2

SKILLBUILDER PRACTICE *Following Chronological Order*

How did the order of events and simultaneous actions shape the progress of the Civil War? The passage below describes a portion of the war in Virginia. Read the passage, then plot the dates and events on the time line at the bottom of the page. (See Skillbuilder Handbook, p. R3.)

The Peninsular Campaign Union General McClellan and his troops landed at the tip of the Virginia peninsula in the spring of 1862. They occupied the city of Yorktown, and then began moving along the York River toward Richmond, hoping to take the Confederate capital. They had drawn within six miles of Richmond when, on May 31, Confederate forces commanded by General Joseph E. Johnston attacked them. The ensuing battle, called the Battle of Fair Oaks, lasted two days and ended when the Confederate troops retreated to Richmond. On the first day of the battle, General Johnston had been wounded. The next day, General Robert E. Lee took his place as commander of the Army of Northern Virginia.

The Valley Campaign Part of the Confederate strategy to save Richmond was to prevent Union reinforcements from reaching McClellan in

Virginia. To that end, Confederate General Stonewall Jackson led a campaign in the Shenandoah Valley to convince Union generals that he was about to attack Washington. From May 4 through June 9, as McClellan was attempting to take Richmond, Jackson pushed his soldiers through the Shenandoah Valley, winning battles and drawing Union troops away from going to McClellan's aid.

After June 9, Jackson's troops joined Lee's army near Richmond. On June 25, the Union and Confederate armies fought in the area around Richmond in what came to be called the Seven Days' Battles. Some of the battles that took place during that time include Gaines Mills on June 27, Savage's Station on June 29, and the last battle, at Malvern Hill on July 1. McClellan's troops then fell back to the James River, and Lee returned to Richmond, which was saved from Union attack.

Spring of 1862
McClellan lands
in Virginia.

July 1, 1862
McClellan is defeated;
Lee returns to Richmond.

SKILLBUILDER PRACTICE *Forming Generalizations*

The decisions by the Supreme Court during the 1870s had a major impact on efforts to make Reconstruction in the South work. What do the decisions and their effects reveal about the influence of the Supreme Court in general? Read the passage below, then answer the questions at the bottom of the page. (See Skillbuilder Handbook, p. R16.)

The *Slaughterhouse* Cases In 1869 the legislature of the state of Louisiana had agreed to give all the slaughterhouse business in New Orleans to one company and to close all the other slaughterhouses. The butchers whose businesses had been closed sued the state for illegally taking away their occupation, in violation of the Fourteenth Amendment guarantee that no state could "abridge the privileges or immunities" of a United States citizen.

The Supreme Court ruled in favor of the Louisiana legislature and against the butchers. Basically, the Court interpreted the Fourteenth Amendment to mean that protection of rights under the amendment applied only to the rights people had because they were citizens of the nation, such as the right to travel safely between two states. The amendment did not apply, the Court said, to the basic civil rights a person acquires by being a citizen of a state. As a result, the federal government was not required to protect those civil rights from the states. The Fourteenth Amendment had been intended to prevent the states from infringing on the rights of former slaves. The Supreme Court's decision nearly nullified that intent.

The Weakening of Reconstruction The ruling in the *Slaughterhouse* cases and in other cases before the Supreme Court in the 1870s signaled the Court's pulling of its support for Reconstruction. State and local officials found numerous loopholes in the laws to limit the rights of African-American men, confirming fears among Northerners that Reconstruction's goal of equality could not be enforced.

Gradually, political support for Reconstruction also dwindled, helped by President Grant's reluctance to use federal power in state and local affairs. Reconstruction officially ended in the South with the political deal known as the Compromise of 1877. By then, Southern Democrats had replaced Republicans in state legislatures and reversed Republican policies, thus limiting the rights and opportunities of free African-American men.

1. What were some short-term effects of the Court's decision in the *Slaughterhouse* cases?

_____

_____

2. What were some long-term effects?

_____

_____

3. How would you generalize about the Supreme Court's influence on other areas of American politics?

_____

_____

REVIEW CHAPTER 4

Section 1

RETEACHING ACTIVITY *The Divisive Politics of Slavery*

───

Finding Main Ideas Choose the best answer for each item. Write the letter of your answer in the blank.

_____ 1. The Compromise of 1850 provided that _____ be admitted as a free state.
    a. New Mexico
    b. Kansas
    c. Nebraska
    d. California

_____ 2. The _____ Party was comprised of numerous groups, including antislavery Whigs and Democrats as well as nativists.
    a. Republican
    b. Free-Soil
    c. Federalist
    d. Know-Nothing

_____ 3. The celebrated _____ debates helped to push the slavery issue to the nation's forefront.
    a. Hayne-Webster
    b. Lincoln-Douglas
    c. Grant-Lee
    d. Brooks-Sumner

_____ 4. The raid on Harpers Ferry made _____ a hero in the North and a villain in the South.
    a. Jefferson Davis
    b. Harriet Tubman
    c. John Brown
    d. Charles Sumner

_____ 5. The _____ in essence repealed the Missouri Compromise by allowing popular sovereignty in territories that had been legally closed to slavery.
    a. Fugitive Slave Act
    b. Compromise of 1850
    c. Kansas-Nebraska Act
    d. Emancipation Proclamation

_____ 6. The president of the Confederacy was _____.
    a. Jefferson Davis
    b. Abraham Lincoln
    c. William Tecumseh Sherman
    d. Stephen Douglas

_____ 7. The *Dred Scott* decision was a victory for _____.
    a. slaves
    b. slaveholders
    c. abolitionists
    d. nativists

_____ 8. The first state to secede from the Union was _____.
    a. Virginia
    b. Tennessee
    c. Georgia
    d. South Carolina

REVIEW
CHAPTER

4

Section 2

RETEACHING ACTIVITY *The Civil War Begins*

Reading Comprehension

After reviewing Section 2, complete each sentence with the appropriate word or words.

prisons	expanded	David Farragut
Red Cross	discrimination	Richmond
split in half	George McClellan	New Orleans
Robert E. Lee	Ulysses S. Grant	blockade
Union	devastated	enlistments

1. A major part of the Union's strategy called for a _____ of Confederate ports.

2. Lincoln responded to the defeat at Bull Run by stepping up _____.

3. In the spring of 1862, a Union naval expedition commanded by _____ captured the city of _____, leaving the Confederacy dangerously close to being _____.

4. The spring of 1862 also saw Confederate General _____ successfully stop Union forces from taking _____, the capital of the Confederacy.

5. Angered that Union forces did not attempt to pursue and defeat Lee's army after the Battle of Antietam, President Lincoln fired his general, _____.

6. The Emancipation Proclamation applied only to enslaved persons outside _____ control.

7. African Americans who served in the Union army faced much _____.

8. A significant percentage of soldiers on both sides died in enemy _____.

9. In general, the war _____ the North's economy and _____ the economy of the South.

10. Civil War nurse Clara Barton went on to found the _____.

Name _____ Date _____

A. Summarizing Complete the chart below by filling in the missing information.

Battle	Date	Victor	Significance
Chancellorsville			
Gettysburg			
Vicksburg			
Richmond			

B. Evaluating *T* in the blank if the statement is true. If the statement is false, write
F in the blank and then write the corrected statement on the line below.

_____ 1. The Civil War greatly increased the power of the federal government.

_____

_____ 2. As a result of the war, the South's economy boomed, while the economy of the North slumped.

_____

_____ 3. The war ushered in the use of ironclad ships, which were superior to the wooden ships of the

       past.

_____

_____ 4. The Thirteenth Amendment abolished slavery in all states in the western territory.

_____

Name _____   Date _____

REVIEW CHAPTER **4**

Section 4

RETEACHING ACTIVITY *Reconstruction and Its Effects*

A. Comparing Complete the graphic below by comparing President Johnson's Reconstruction plan with that of the Radical Republicans.

```
                        ┌──────────────────────┐
                        │  RECONSTRUCTION PLAN │
                        └──────────────────────┘
                          /                  \
     ┌──────────────────────┐        ┌──────────────────────┐
     │ PRESIDENT JOHNSON    │        │ RADICAL REPUBLICANS  │
     │                      │        │                      │
     │                      │        │                      │
     │                      │        │                      │
     │                      │        │                      │
     │                      │        │                      │
     └──────────────────────┘        └──────────────────────┘
```

War with Mexico   Horace Greeley   New Mexico
California   James Marshall   slavery
War for Texas Independence   land   Missouri

B. Finding Main Ideas Choose the word that most accurately completes the sentences below.

Amnesty Act   redemption   Panic of 1873
African American   Anaconda Plan   Ten Percent Plan
Enforcement Acts   women   Reconstruction Act

1. Ulysses S. Grant won the presidency in 1868 with the help of _____ voters.

2. Southerners referred to their resumption of power in the region as _____.

3. In May of 1872, Congress passed the _____, which returned the right to vote and hold office to numerous Confederates.

4. An economic crisis triggered by the _____ helped to weaken support for Reconstruction.

5. President Lincoln's procedure for reunifying the nation was known as the _____.

REVIEW CHAPTER **4**

Section 4

GEOGRAPHY APPLICATION: HUMAN-ENVIRONMENT INTERACTIONS
Slave Populations in the United States

*Directions: Read the paragraphs below and study the map and chart carefully.
Then answer the questions that follow.*

At the outbreak of the Civil War, the vast majority of African Americans in the United States were slaves living in the rural areas of the South. Even after the Union victory, however, most African Americans remained in the South. During World War I, the distribution of African Americans began to change. Drawn by job opportunities, they began to move to the industrial cities of the North and Northeast. In recent years, though, large numbers of African Americans have joined the migration to the Sunbelt, the region made up of the Southwestern and Western states.

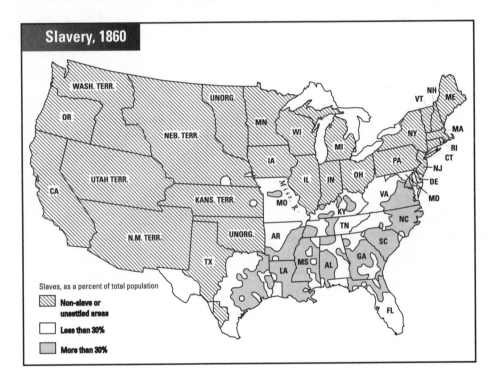

States with the Largest African-American Populations, 1990			
1. New York	2,859,000	7. North Carolina	1,456,000
2. California	2,209,000	8. Louisiana	1,299,000
3. Texas	2,022,000	9. Michigan	1,292,000
4. Florida	1,760,000	10. Maryland	1,190,000
5. Georgia	1,747,000	11. Virginia	1,163,000
6. Illinois	1,694,000	12. Ohio	1,155,000

Interpreting Text and Visuals

1. List the 14 states that had areas with a slave population of more than 30 percent in 1860. _____

   _____

   _____

   _____

   _____

   _____

2. List the four free states west of the Mississippi River. _____

   _____

3. In contrast to many other states, Missouri, Kentucky, and Maryland had a difficult time deciding which side to join during the Civil War. Why do you think this was so?

   _____

   _____

   _____

4. Study the map and the table. Then list the states that had both a substantial slave population in 1860 and a large African-American population in 1990. _____

   _____

   _____

5. Name the six states that had African-American populations of more than 1.5 million in 1990. _____

   _____

6. Despite the history of slavery in the South, many free African Americans chose to stay there after the Civil War. What factors do you think might have caused them to make this choice?

   _____

   _____

   _____

   _____

Name _____ Date _____

REVIEW CHAPTER
4
Section 2

OUTLINE MAP *The States Choose Sides*

A. Review textbook pages 165 and 170, paying particular attention to the Historical Spotlight about secession and the Civil War map. Then on the accompanying outline map label the states and color or shade each of the three areas identified in the key. (For a complete map of the states, see textbook pages A6–A7.) Finally, label the Mississippi and Ohio rivers and draw the position of the Union blockade using the symbol shown in the key.

B. After completing the map, use it to answer the following questions.

1. How many states made up the Confederacy? _____

2. What were the slave states that did not secede and join the Confederacy? _____

_____

   Which one was not officially a state at the beginning of the war? _____

3. Which major river split the Confederacy into two parts? _____

4. What are the approximate lengths in miles of the Confederate and of the Union coastlines? _____

_____

   Imagine that there had been no blockade of the Confederate coastline. How might such a situation have influenced the outcome of the Civil War? _____

_____

_____

_____

_____

5. In mid-1863 the Union gained control of the entire length of the Mississippi River. What strategic advantage did this give the Union? _____

_____

_____

_____

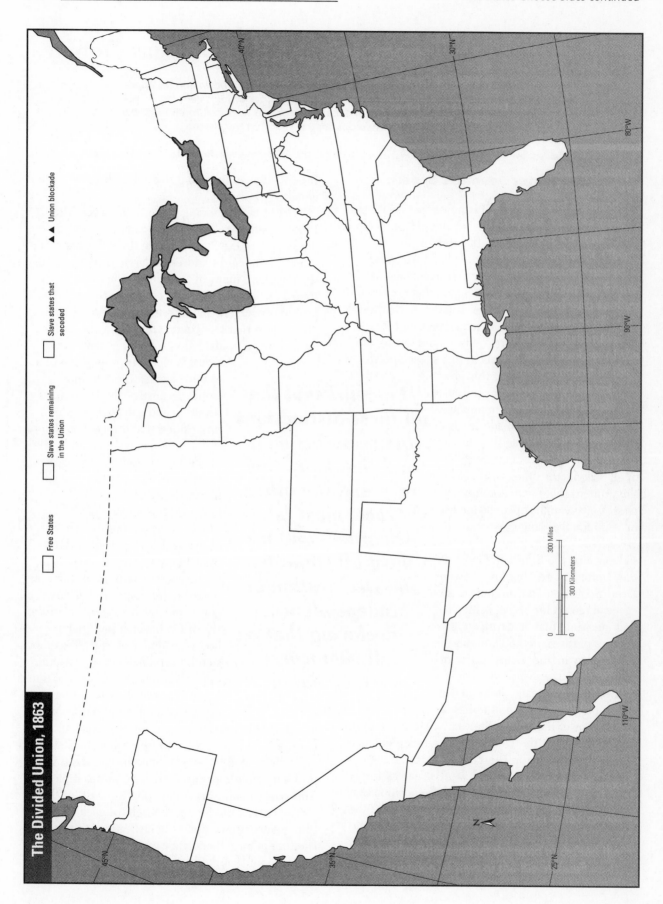

The Divided Union, 1863

Free States

Slave states remaining in the Union

Slave states that seceded

▲ ▲ Union blockade

300 Miles

300 Kilometers

REVIEW
CHAPTER

4

Section 1

PRIMARY SOURCE *from* The Lincoln-Douglas Debates

During the Illinois senatorial campaign in 1858, Abraham Lincoln and his opponent, Senator Stephen A. Douglas, took part in a series of joint debates. As you read this excerpt from the seventh debate, which was held in Alton on October 15, compare and contrast the two candidates' views on the issues.

from **Senator Douglas's Speech**

Ladies and Gentlemen: It is now nearly four months since the canvass between Mr. Lincoln and myself commenced. On the 16th of June the Republican Convention assembled at Springfield and nominated Mr. Lincoln as their candidate for the United States Senate, and he, on that occasion, delivered a speech in which he laid down what he understood to be the Republican creed, and the platform on which he proposed to stand during the contest. The principal points in that speech of Mr. Lincoln's were: First, that this government could not endure permanently divided into free and slave States, as our fathers made it; that they must all become free or all become slave; all become one thing, or all become the other,—otherwise this Union could not continue to exist. I give you his opinions almost in the identical language he used. His second proposition was a crusade against the Supreme Court of the United States because of the Dred Scott decision, urging as an especial reason for his opposition to that decision that it deprived the negroes of the rights and benefits of that clause in the Constitution of the United States which guarantees to the citizens of each State all the rights, privileges, and immunities of the citizens of the several States. . . . He insisted, in that speech, that the Declaration of Independence included the negro in the clause asserting that all men were created equal and went so far as to say that if one man was allowed to take the position that it did not include the negro, others might take the position that it did not include other men. He said that all these distinctions between this man and that man, this race and the other race, must be discarded, and we must all stand by the Declaration of

[Lincoln] said that all these distinctions between this man and that man, this race and the other race, must be discarded, and we must all stand by the Declaration of Independence, declaring that all men were created equal.

Independence, declaring that all men were created equal.

The issue thus being made up between Mr. Lincoln and myself on three points, we went before the people of the State. During the following seven weeks . . . he and I addressed large assemblages of the people in many of the central counties. In my speeches I confined myself closely to those three positions which he had taken, controverting his proposition that this Union could not exist as our fathers made it, divided into free and slave States, controverting his proposition of a crusade against the Supreme Court because of the Dred Scott decision, and controverting his proposition that the Declaration of Independence included and meant the negroes as well as the white men, when it declared all men to be created equal. . . . I took up Mr. Lincoln's three propositions in my several speeches, analyzed them, and pointed out what I believed to be the radical errors contained in them. First, in regard to his doctrine that this government was in violation of the law of God, which says that a house divided against itself cannot stand, I repudiated it as a slander upon the immortal framers of our Constitution. I then said, I have often repeated, and now again assert, that in my opinion our government can endure forever, divided into free and slave States as our fathers made it,—each State having the right to prohibit, abolish, or sustain slavery, just as it pleases. This government was made upon the basis of the sovereignty of the States, the right of each State to regulate its own domestic institutions to suit itself. . . . Our fathers knew when they made the government that the laws and institutions which were well adapted to the Green Mountains of

Vermont were unsuited to the rice plantations of South Carolina. They knew then, as well as we know now, that the laws and institutions which would be well adapted to the beautiful prairies of Illinois would not be suited to the mining regions of California. They knew that in a republic as broad as this, having such a variety of soil, climate, and interest, there must necessarily be a corresponding variety of local laws,—the policy and institutions of each State adapted to its condition and wants. For this reason this Union was established on the right of each State to do as it pleased on the question of slavery, and every other question; and the various States were not allowed to complain of, much less interfere with, the policy of their neighbors. . . .

from **Mr. Lincoln's Reply**

I have stated upon former occasions, and I may as well state again, what I understand to be the real issue in this controversy between Judge Douglas and myself. . . . The real issue in this controversy— the one pressing upon every mind—is the senti- ment on the part of one class that looks upon the institution of slavery *as a wrong,* and of another class that *does not look* upon it as a wrong. The sentiment that contemplates the institution of slav- ery in this country as a wrong is the sentiment of the Republican party. It is the sentiment around which all their actions, all their arguments, circle, from which all their propositions radiate. They look upon it as being a moral, social, and political wrong; and while they contemplate it as such, they nevertheless have due regard for its actual exis- tence among us, and the difficulties of getting rid of it in any satisfactory way, and to all the constitu- tional obligations thrown about it. . . . I have said, and I repeat it here, that if there be a man amongst us who does not think that the institution of slavery is wrong in any one of the aspects of which I have spoken, he is misplaced, and ought not to be with us. And if there be a man amongst us who is so impatient of it as a wrong as to disregard its actual presence among us and the difficulty of getting rid of it suddenly in a satisfactory way, and to disregard the constitutional obligations thrown about it, that man is misplaced if he is on our platform. We dis-

claim sympathy with him in practical action. He is not placed properly with us.

On this subject of treating it as a wrong, and limiting its spread, let me say a word. Has anything ever threatened the existence of this Union save and except this very institution of slavery? What is it that we hold dear amongst us? Our own liberty and prosperity. What has ever threatened our liberty and prosperity, save and except this institution of slavery? If this is true, how do you propose to improve the condition of things by enlarging slav- ery,—by spreading it out and making it bigger? You may have a wen or cancer upon your person, and not be able to cut it out, lest you bleed to death; but surely it is no way to cure it, to engraft it and spread it over your whole body. That is no proper way of treating what you regard a wrong. You see this peaceful way of dealing with it as a wrong,— restricting the spread of it, and not allowing it to go into new countries where it has not already existed. That is the peaceful way, the old-fashioned way, the way in which the fathers themselves set us the example. . . .

That is the real issue. That is the issue that will continue in this country when these poor tongues of Judge Douglas and myself shall be silent. It is the eternal struggle between these two principles— right and wrong—throughout the world. They are the two principles that have stood face to face from the beginning of time, and will ever continue to struggle.

from Henry Steele Commager, ed., *Documents of American History* (New York: F. S. Crofts & Co., 1947), 351–358.

Activity Options

1. Work with a partner to re-create the Lincoln- Douglas debates. Using this excerpt or one of the other six joint debates, role-play either Douglas or Lincoln and present the debate to the class.
2. Use information in this excerpt as well as in your textbook to write two campaign slogans—one for Douglas and one for Lincoln—to express their views on slavery. Then share your slogans with classmates.

PRIMARY SOURCE The Emancipation Proclamation

President Abraham Lincoln issued the Emancipation Proclamation on January 1, 1863. As you read the proclamation, consider its impact on slaves and slaveholders.

Whereas on the 22nd day of September, A.D. 1862, a proclamation was issued by the President of the United States, containing among other things, the following, to wit:

"That on the 1st day of January, A.D. 1863, all persons held as slaves within any State or designated part of a State the people whereof shall then be in rebellion against the United States shall be then, thenceforward, and forever free; and the executive government of the United States, including the military and naval authority thereof, will recognize and maintain the freedom of such persons and will do no act or acts to repress such persons, or any of them, in any efforts they may make for their actual freedom.

"That the executive will on the 1st day of January aforesaid, by proclamation, designate the States and parts of States, if any, in which the people thereof, respectively, shall then be in rebellion against the United States; and the fact that any State or the people thereof shall on that day be in good faith represented in the Congress of the United States by members chosen thereto at elections wherein a majority of the qualified voters of such States shall have participated shall, in the absence of strong countervailing testimony, be deemed conclusive evidence that such State and the people thereof are not then in rebellion against the United States."

Now, therefore, I, Abraham Lincoln, President of the United States, by virtue of the power in me vested as Commander-in-Chief of the Army and Navy of the United States in time of actual armed rebellion against the authority and government of the United States, and as a fit and necessary war measure for suppressing said rebellion, do, on this 1st day of January, A.D. 1863, and in accordance with my purpose to do so, publicly proclaimed for the full period of one hundred days from the first day above mentioned, order and designate as the States and parts of States wherein the people thereof, respectively, are this day in rebellion against the United States the following, to wit:

Arkansas, Texas, Louisiana (except the parishes of St. Bernard, Plaquemines, Jefferson, St. John, St. Charles, St. James, Ascension, Assumption, Terrebone,

Lafourche, St. Mary, St. Martin, and Orleans, including the city of New Orleans), Mississippi, Alabama, Florida, Georgia, South Carolina, North Carolina, and Virginia (except the forty-eight counties designated as West Virginia, and also the counties of Berkeley, Accomac, Northhampton, Elizabeth City, York, Princess Anne, and Norfolk, including the cities of Norfolk and Portsmouth), and which excepted parts are for the present left precisely as if this proclamation were not issued.

And by virtue of the power and for the purpose aforesaid, I do order and declare that all persons held as slaves within said designated States and parts of States are, and henceforward shall be, free; and that the Executive Government of the United States, including the military and naval authorities thereof, will recognize and maintain the freedom of said persons.

And I hereby enjoin upon the people so declared to be free to abstain from all violence, unless in necessary self-defense; and I recommend to them that, in all cases when allowed, they labor faithfully for reasonable wages.

And I further declare and make known that such persons of suitable condition will be received into the armed service of the United States to garrison forts, positions, stations, and other places, and to man vessels of all sorts in said service.

And upon this act, sincerely believed to be an act of justice, warranted by the Constitution upon military necessity, I invoke the considerate judgment of mankind and the gracious favor of Almighty God.

from *U.S. Statutes at Large*, Vol. XII, 1268–9. Reprinted in Henry Steele Commager, ed., *Documents of American History*, 3rd ed., Vol. I (New York: F. S. Crofts & Co., 1947), 420–421.

Activity Options

1. In a two-column chart, list the possible moral and military effects of the Emancipation Proclamation. Share your chart with your classmates.
2. With a small group of classmates, paraphrase the two paragraphs within the quotation marks. Then read your paraphrase aloud to the class.

PRIMARY SOURCE On the Burning of
Columbia, South Carolina

*Columbia, South Carolina, was devastated by fire on February 17, 1865.
Although the fire was attributed to General William T. Sherman and his Union
troops, Sherman claimed that he was not responsible. Who or what does
Sherman blame for Columbia's burning in this excerpt from his report on the
Campaign of the Carolinas?*

In anticipation of the occupation of the city, I had made written orders to General Howard touching the conduct of the troops. These were to destroy, absolutely, all arsenals and public property not needed for our own use, as well as all railroads, depots, and machinery useful in war to an enemy, but to spare all dwellings, colleges, schools, asylums, and harmless private property. I was the first to cross the pontoon bridge, and in company with General Howard rode into the city. The day was clear, but a perfect tempest of wind was raging. The brigade of Colonel Stone was already in the city, and was properly posted. Citizens and soldiers were on the streets, and general good order prevailed. General Wade Hampton, who commanded the Confederate rear-guard of cavalry, had, in anticipation of our capture of Columbia, ordered that all cotton, public and private, should be moved into the streets and fired, to prevent our making use of it. Bales were piled everywhere, the rope and bagging cut, and tufts of cotton were blown about in the wind, lodged in the trees and against houses, so as to resemble a snow storm. Some of these piles of cotton were burning, especially one in the very heart of the city, near the Court-house, but the fire was partially subdued by the labor of our soldiers. . . .

Before one single public building had been fired by order, the smoldering fires, set by Hampton's order, were rekindled by the wind, and communicated to the buildings around. About dark they began to spread, and got beyond the control of the brigade on duty within the city. The whole of Wood's division was brought in, but it was found impossible to check the flames, which, by midnight, had become unmanageable, and raged until about

four A.M., when the wind subsiding, they were got under control. I was up nearly all night, and saw Generals Howard, Logan, Woods, and others, laboring to save houses and protect families thus suddenly deprived of shelter, and of bedding and wearing apparel. I disclaim on the part of my army any agency in this fire, but on the contrary, claim that we saved what of Columbia remains unconsumed. And without hesitation, I charge General Wade Hampton with having burned his own city of Columbia, not with a malicious intent, or as the manifestations of a silly "Roman stoicism," but from folly and want of sense, in filling it with lint, cotton, and tinder. Our officers and men on duty worked well to extinguish the flames; but others not on duty, including the officers who had long been imprisoned there, rescued by us, may have assisted in spreading the fire after it had once begun, and may have indulged in unconcealed joy to see the ruin of the capital of South Carolina.

from "Report of General Sherman on the Campaign of the Carolinas, April 4, 1865" in F. Moore, ed., *The Rebellion Record*, Vol. IX, 377.

Discussion Questions

1. According to Sherman's report, who or what was responsible for the burning of Columbia, South Carolina?
2. According to this excerpt, what role did the Union army play after the fire in Columbia began on February 17, 1865?
3. Do you believe Sherman's account of the burning of Columbia? Why or why not? Cite evidence from your textbook to support your opinion.

REVIEW CHAPTER 4

Section 4

PRIMARY SOURCE *from* An Inquiry on the Condition of the South

Congress established the Joint Select Committee to investigate reports of violence and intimidation in the South. On August 4, 1871, the committee took this testimony from Henry B. Whitfield, the mayor of Columbus, Mississippi. What does Whitfield's testimony reveal about conditions in Mississippi during Reconstruction?

QUESTION. This committee is charged with inquiring into the condition of affairs in Mississippi and other States, especially in reference to the safety of property and life, and the due execution of the law. State anything you know on that subject.

ANSWER. I consider that in the counties in Eastern Mississippi particularly, and on the Alabama line, and in North Mississippi, on the Tennessee line, there is considerable insecurity to liberty of person, and in some instances to life, unless a party espouses certain opinions.

QUESTION. What opinions do you mean?

ANSWER. I mean that if a white man, an old citizen of the county, is known to be a member of the republican party, the people are very intolerant toward him; and if a northern man who has come there is a republican they are a little worse toward him; and toward the black people, unless they are willing to vote as the people there desire them to vote, they are very intolerant. . . .

QUESTION. Take first your own county of Lowndes, and state the condition of things there.

ANSWER. . . . Back as far as the year 1868 was the first time that we had any indications there of any organizations which appeared to be for improper purposes—for the purpose of controlling opinion or making people do as they wanted them to do. Such organizations then existed, being organized during the campaign of 1868—at the time of the election for the convention in the State. During 1869 and a part of 1870, we did not hear of anything of the kind to any extent in Lowndes County. But last February the thing seemed to have broken loose again with every indication of violence, and to a very outrageous extent in the northeastern part of the county.

QUESTION. The part of the county bordering on the Alabama line?

ANSWER. Yes, sir. . . . I will state that the first outbreak which occurred was in the latter part of February of the present year. The victim was a negro named James Hicks. . . . It was charged that . . . he had used some improper language in regard to some white ladies of the neighborhood; and these people determined, I suppose, that he should suffer for it. He had moved down some seven miles below that, into another neighborhood. They found out where he lived, followed him down there, and took him out one night. From the best information I could get, there were from one hundred to one hundred and twenty disguised men, who were armed heavily. They took him out into the public road and whipped him. The statements of the witnesses varied considerably as to the amount of whipping he received. The lowest estimate that I heard was three hundred lashes; some of the black people who were present thought it was as high as one thousand. I have no doubt myself, from the man's appearance two days afterward, and from the evidence in the case, that he was very severely beaten.

from *Testimony Taken by the Joint Select Committee to Inquire into the Condition of Affairs in the Late Insurrectionary States.* Reprinted in Louis M. Hacker, ed., *The Shaping of the American Tradition* (New York: Columbia University Press, 1947) 647–651.

Activity Options

1. Imagine yourself as a member of the Joint Select Committee. Write a list of questions that you might want to ask witnesses about conditions in the South during Reconstruction.
2. With a small group of classmates, role-play the questioning of Whitfield by the Joint Select Committee.
3. Based on your reading of Chapter 4, list two or three witnesses that you think the Joint Select Committee could have called to testify.

REVIEW CHAPTER

4

Section 4

LITERATURE SELECTION *from* Jubilee

by Margaret Walker

Jubilee is based on the true story of Margaret Walker's great-grandmother, Vyry, during the years before the Civil War through Reconstruction. In this excerpt, Vyry, her husband, Innis, and her children Jim, Minna, and Harry are home-steading in Alabama after the war. They work for awhile at the Jacobsons' house and sawmill before putting in the crops on their new farm. In keeping with the setting of this novel, some of the white characters use offensive racial epithets.

Spring of 1869 was a turbulent spring in Alabama. There were Negro soldiers in the streets of Troy as well as many northern white strangers. The local white people and the northern whites clashed and there were scuffles among the Negroes and between the Negroes and whites. Vyry and Innis kept thinking how glad they were that they lived on the outskirts of town on top of one of its many hills. They went back and forth to the Jacobsons throughout the month of March and meanwhile they were going on Sunday nights to church meeting.

The question of a new Negro school had created some controversy. The whites wanted to know where the money was coming for "nigger" children to read books when there were fields that needed to be worked, sawmills, and turpentine camps that were going idle. Mr. Jacobson [the white owner of the sawmill where Innis works] told Innis he didn't know how it was all going to work out, that they should be careful. Innis told Vyry that it was all right for Minna, but he thought it might be a mistake to send Jim to school.

"Why?" asked Vyry.

"He's old enough to work, that's why."

"But he got a right to learn, too, ain't he?"

"That ain't the point."

"What is the point?"

"The point is we needs him to help work."

"I wants him to go to school."

"Well, the white folks is saying . . ."

"I don't care what the white folks is saying. I wants my chilluns to learn to read and write."

"Well, they is agin it."

The subject became a sore topic even between Vyry and Innis. When the fifty cents tax was levied, the white folks claimed the Negroes would not pay,

and Innis said, "We ain't got the money."

"We is got the money, Innis Brown, and you knows it."

"But we can't afford it."

"What else can we afford more'n book learning for your younguns?" And, stricken by the conflict, she looked at him and he dropped his eyes.

April came and time to leave the Jacobsons and Vyry was surprised to see that Mrs. Jacobson had not expected it, did not like it, and was not only bitter but almost nasty about it.

"You mean you're going to stop cooking for us now that you've got yourself a house and a farm?"

"Well, ma'am, I figgers my husband needs me to help work the place."

"What about Jim? Can't he help him?"

Vyry felt a pang of fear, but she continued to look steadily at Mrs. Jacobson while she spoke, "Yes'm, Jim can help, but I figered whilst all the spring plowing and planting's going on they can't hardly manage all by themselves."

"Can't Minna keep the baby and look after the house?"

"Yes'm, she can," and now Vyry was twisting her apron in her hands, and her agitation must have been visible to her employer at this point.

"Oh, I know, you want them to go to school, is that it?" And Vyry could tell from the accusing tone of Mrs. Jacobson's voice that she really didn't like the idea even though it was she who had given Minna her first book.

"Well, ma'am, I was thinking you more'n anybody else would understand."

"Yes, I do understand. I understand how you colored people don't want to work the way you useta. What's more you won't work the way you useta. You expect everything to come dropping in your laps, houses and land and schools and churches

The question of a new Negro school had created some controversy.

and money, and you want to leave the white people holding the bag. We've done everything we can for you, my husband and I . . ."

"Yes'm, you sho is," said Vyry miserably trying to avoid a big misunderstanding by interrupting, "and we appreciates it, ma'am, we does."

"It doesn't look like it now."

"I wasn't planning on quitting working for you for good, Missus Jacobson. I just wants to help him get the cotton and corn and taters in the ground."

"Oh, yes, you want everything at your convenience and none at mine. You take off any time at all and you need not come back." And Vyry, with her head bowed, sorrowfully turned away.

One April morning Vyry and Innis and Jim were hard at work in the field. It was nearly noon and they would soon stop working and go to the house for dinner. Minna was in the house with Harry. She could clean the house and wash the dishes and tend Vyry's cooking pots while the others were in the field. When Harry was asleep she tried to figure out the words in her picture book which Mrs. Jacobson had given her. She had worn it hard and thin and she fussed with Jim if his hands were dirty and messed up her book while he tried to read it in the evenings. They would have fought over that book had it not been for Vyry. This was a bright, sunshiny morning, a Friday, and although Minna did not exactly understand the difference in all the days yet, she was learning. She knew it was Friday because Vyry kept track of church meeting night and there were two more nights before Sunday. Minna put down her book and went to look at the pots on the stove. Standing in the back door were three half-grown white boys or young men, and they were walking into the house. Minna was startled and stepped back toward the room where Harry was sleeping.

"Hey, nigger-gal, what you cooking?" And one of the boys moved toward Minna, while the other two giggled. Minna backed quickly into the bedroom and grabbed Harry. Awakened suddenly from a nap, he hollered.

"Make him shut up, nigger-gal, or I'll cut his

> *Standing in the back door were three half-grown white boys or young men, and they were walking into the house. Minna was startled and stepped back toward the room where Harry was sleeping.*

black throat with my razor."

They were still coming in the room and Minna, now frightened out of her wits, had Harry in her arms and was backing into a corner. When he screamed again and she saw the boy flick the razor she put her hand over Harry's mouth and muffled his sound. The boys were still grinning, and one said, "We wants a drink of water, nigger-gal, come on outside and give it to us." But they stood blocking her path and when she made an effort to move they laughed and moved in closer. Now the third boy looked at his friends and then back at Minna and Harry, and pointing his finger from one to the other he began to mimic,

Eeny, meeny, minie, moe,
Catch a nigger by his toe,
If he holler let him go.
Eeny, meeny, minie, moe.

And they were laughing loudly when suddenly coming through the house were Innis, Vyry, and Jim. The boys were startled when they looked up and saw three their size. One of them wanted to stand his ground and get ugly, but after a moment's hard silence another said, "Come on yall, let's git outa this nigger house. It stinks." And laughing loudly again, they ran out. Minna was near the point of hysteria and she collapsed in Vyry's arms screaming. "Maw, oh Maw!"

Innis and Jim were unable to utter a word but they fully understood Minna's terror and the whole family was stunned into silence. Saturday morning Vyry did not go into the field with Innis and Jim. She knew she could not leave Minna alone in the house again, even though they were so near.

"I'm just thankful it wasn't no worse than it was."

"It was bad enough, Maw. They nearabouts scared me to death."

"I knows they did. Your Paw and me keeps wondering what they come up here for in the first place."

"I guess they was just out in the woods and wanted water, so they come over here and then they seen me here by myself and started meddling."

"I dunno. I just don't know."

Vyry and Minna were cooking and baking for Sunday as well as Saturday.

"We's gwine have the new preacher for dinner tomorrow and then we's all gwine to town for evening meeting."

"All us?"

"Yeah, your Paw says so."

Although Vyry worked hard all day scrubbing and cleaning and cooking and baking, and sometimes singing from long force of habit, she was deeply troubled over the boys' intrusion on Friday. She wanted to tell somebody like the Jacobsons, but she knew Mrs. Jacobson was still angry. "She'll just hafta git over it, I reckons."

"What did you say, Maw?"

"Nothing, Minna. I was just thinking."

Sunday was a merry day. The new house shone with Vyry's best. Everybody was happy to have company. Once, when Jim was gulping down chicken and dumplings faster than seemed company manners, Innis roughly reproved him, "Sirrah, there boy! Ain't nobody running you no race. This food ain't gwine no place." But to the preacher he said, "Eat hearty, Reverend, if they ain't enough my wife'll cook some more."

And they laughed, for Vyry always had more than enough.

They were climbing the hill that night between nine and ten o'clock. Innis was riding Harry on his back. Vyry was still deep in the mood of the meeting, hearing the singing and the preaching and the stirring testimonies. She could still feel the intense joy of the song she was humming,

> Tell me how did you feel when you come out
>   the wilderness?
> Come out the wilderness,
> Come out the wilderness,
> Tell me how did you feel when you come out
>   the wilderness
> Leaning on the Lawd?

She had Minna's hand in hers, and the little girl was looking up at the sky full of stars and the house at the top of the hill that was home, when suddenly she cried out, "Look, Maw! Paw, looka-there!"

It was happening so suddenly they hardly real-

They saw a half-dozen white-sheeted and hooded figures, some on horseback, some holding horses, and others busy on the ground.

ized the stunning impact. They saw a half-dozen white-sheeted and hooded figures, some on horseback, some holding horses, and others busy on the ground. Then they saw them hoist a huge rough cross-like structure tall as a tree and flaming with fire, and it rose up on the hill against their house. Suddenly they felt the earth rock under their feet, and they smelled the strong fumes of kerosene oil, and they heard an explosive noise break forth on the spring night, while expertly directed flames licked their beautiful new house and it burst into a roaring fire. As the blaze leaped up the white-sheeted riders galloped away and vanished into the spring night.

Innis began running and Vyry, with her heart in her throat, tried to run, but she felt herself stumbling forward heavily and weighted as though in a dream. Jim and Minna were running and screaming and thinking this must be a nightmare and not their brand-new house with windows from the mill. Innis was fighting the flames to pull out Vyry's new churn, her chest, and her spinning wheel. They were blackened with smoke and the smoke was choking him, so they were all that he managed to save.

Activity Options

1. In a two-column chart, list the negative and positive aspects of Reconstruction that Vyry and her family experience in this excerpt from *Jubilee*. Then share your chart with the class.

2. Write a diary entry about Reconstruction from the point of view of one of these characters. Remember to keep in character as you write down thoughts and feelings. To clarify how each of these characters might have reacted to Reconstruction, draw on information in your textbook.

3. Write a factual newspaper story about the fire that destroys the family's home. Be sure to explain what happened, when it took place, where it happened, who was involved, and why it occurred. Post your news story in the classroom.

REVIEW CHAPTER 4

Section 1

AMERICAN LIVES Harriet Tubman
Conductor to Freedom

"Excepting John Brown . . . I know of no one who has willingly encountered more perils and hardships to serve our enslaved people than you have."—
Frederick Douglass, letter to Harriet Tubman (1868)

Herself an escaped slave, Harriet Tubman risked her life countless times by returning to the South to free others from slavery. She became known as "the Moses of her people," because she led so many from captivity to the promise of the North.

Harriet Tubman (c. 1820–1913) was born around 1820 on the eastern shore of Maryland. When she was six, her master hired her out to another family to work. She was uncooperative, though, and was sent back. After another failed effort to hire her out, she was made a field hand. When only 13, she blocked an overseer from pursuing an escaping slave. He hurled a two-pound weight that hit Tubman, fracturing her skull. Until the end of her life, she suffered occasional blackouts as a result of the blow.

She recovered from the incident and later joined her father in being hired out to a builder. She worked hard, performing heavy labor that normally was done by men. She preferred such work to being in the kitchen or doing cleaning. She became strong and tough. She married John Tubman during this period.

When the plantation owner died, slaves were sold because the estate was struggling. One day in 1849, Tubman was told that she and her brothers had been sold. Determined not to be sent further South, she escaped that night.

Aided by the Underground Railroad, Tubman made it to Philadelphia and began to work in hotels. Visiting the Philadelphia Vigilance Committee, which helped runaways, she learned that her brother-in-law was planning to come North with his wife, her sister, and their child. Tubman returned South to lead them to freedom. The next year she brought out a brother and his family. Later she returned for her husband, but he had remarried and chose not to leave. Tubman led out 11 others instead.

Throughout the 1850s, Tubman returned to the South almost twenty times. She let slaves know that she was nearby with a simple secret message:

"Moses is here." She brought anywhere from sixty to three hundred slaves to the North–among them her parents. She became notorious throughout the South, where the reward for her capture went as high as $40,000.

In the North, Tubman became friends with the leading abolitionists, including Wendell Phillips and Frederick Douglass. She was visited by John Brown. He had a plan to free large numbers of slaves and hoped to take advantage of Tubman's detailed knowledge of geography and conditions in the South. At about this time, she also began to make public appearances, describing the evils of slavery and telling the stories of her rescue voyages.

Tubman was saddened by the collapse of Brown's plan. When the Civil War broke out, she took direct action by helping the Union army in South Carolina. She served as a spy and a scout, going behind Confederate lines to gather information from slaves. She also worked as a nurse and helped African Americans who had escaped Confederate control.

After the war's end and her husband's death, she remarried. She lived on a farm sold to her for a small amount by William Seward, prominent New York Republican and Abraham Lincoln's secretary of state. She devoted herself to helping others. She started the Harriet Tubman Home for Indigent Aged Negroes to help older former slaves. She campaigned to establish schools in the South for the now-freed African Americans. For many years Tubman tried to persuade Congress to grant her a pension for her work during the war. It was finally approved in 1897.

Questions

1. Why was the route taken by escaping slaves called the Underground Railroad?
2. Why was such a high reward placed on Tubman?
3. In the 1850s, Tubman had a home in St. Catharines, a town in Canada near Buffalo, New York. Why did she lead escaped slaves there?

REVIEW CHAPTER **4**

Section 4

AMERICAN LIVES # Thaddeus Stevens
Passionate Man of Principle

"[If members of Congress would] fling away ambition and realize that every human being, however lowly-born or degraded by fortune, is your equal and that every inalienable right which belongs to you belongs also to him, truth and righteousness will spread over the land."—Thaddeus Stevens, last speech in Congress (1868)

Thaddeus Stevens devoted his congressional life to removing slavery, which he called "a curse, a shame, and a crime." Once that goal was achieved, he labored to win equal rights for African Americans. He accomplished these goals because he was a skilled lawyer and legislator and tireless in his efforts.

Born in Vermont, Stevens (1792–1868) grew up poor and lacking a father, who either died or left his family when he was very young. He applied himself in school, however, and after attending Dartmouth College settled in Pennsylvania. He became a lawyer. Living near Maryland—a slave state—Stevens saw African Americans taken to court as fugitive slaves. He defended many of them, frequently winning the person's freedom.

He was generous with money. Stevens often took no fee for his defense of fugitive slaves. He once used his savings to purchase the freedom of a man about to be taken south as a fugitive. During the Civil War, Confederate raiders destroyed an iron works he owned. Stevens sent money to the families who lost income when the works shut down.

He was elected to the Pennsylvania legislature in 1833. He became known for his legislative skill; his passionate, sometimes angry speeches; and his defense of principle. He won passage of a law that made education free throughout the state. When opponents tried to overturn it, he criticized the move as an effort by the wealthy to suppress the poor. He refused to sign the new Pennsylvania constitution of 1837 because only whites were allowed to vote.

After a brief retirement, Stevens returned to public life, this time in the U.S. House of Representatives. He began to push the antislavery cause with energy and his sharp tongue. He worked against the Compromise of 1850 and the Fugitive Slave Law. His hatred of slavery became anger at Southerners. No polite debater, he blasted Southern representatives as slave-drivers—and also condemned Northern representatives who did not work against slavery.

During and just after the Civil War, he was perhaps the most powerful member of the House of Representatives. He urged aggressive prosecution of the war and lashed out when he felt Abraham Lincoln was not taking strong enough measures. He dismissed Lincoln's plan for emancipation as "diluted milk and water gruel." At the same time, he remembered his commitment to the poor. In arguing for the income tax needed to fund the war, he promised it would be a progressive tax: "No one will be affected by the provisions of this bill whose living depends solely on his manual labor."

After the Civil War, Stevens used his power to punish the South, end slavery, and ensure African-American equality before the law. "The foundation of [Southern] institutions . . . must be broken up and relaid, or all our blood and treasure have been spent in vain," he said. He bitterly opposed Andrew Johnson's mild Reconstruction plan. To combat this plan, he got Congress to create a joint committee on reconstruction, which he dominated. He pushed passage of the Fourteenth Amendment, which ended slavery; the Civil Rights Act of 1866; and the Fifteenth Amendment, which gave African Americans the right to vote.

Growing increasingly ill, Stevens led the effort to impeach Andrew Johnson. A few months after the Senate trial ended with Johnson a one-vote survivor, Stevens died. Following his wishes, he was buried in an African-American cemetery.

Questions

1. How does the quotation at the top of the page reflect Stevens's actions during his life?
2. Would Stevens's style of debate be likely to persuade opponents to accept his ideas?
3. Stevens judged his life a failure. Would you agree? Why or why not?

UNIT
1
Activities

THEMATIC REVIEW *Beginnings Through Reconstruction*

These activities will help you explore the large issues that have influenced the course of American history. You might want to add these activities—or photographs and written descriptions of them—to your theme portfolio.

IMMIGRATION AND MIGRATION Making a Time Line Use newsprint or computer paper to create a wall-sized time line showing the movements of people into North America. You will need to find a way to compress the centuries at the start of your time line and to provide more detail for the later centuries. You may wish to add to the time line throughout the course.

AMERICA IN WORLD AFFAIRS Presenting a Skit Imagine that George Washington returns to life to discover that the United States has just signed the Treaty of Guadalupe Hidalgo. Work with several classmates to write and perform a skit called "What Would Washington Say?" Include at least one character who summarizes changes in foreign affairs since Washington's death in 1799. Begin your research into Washington's point of view by thinking about these words from his farewell address in 1796:

> *Cultivate peace and harmony with all. . . . The great rule of conduct for us in regard to foreign nations is . . . to have with them as little political connection as possible.*

CULTURAL DIVERSITY AND THE NATIONAL IDENTITY Creating a Map Use an opaque projector to draw an outline map of the United States on a large piece of posterboard. Then create a pictorial map showing some of the cultural influences on the various regions of the United States.

STATES' RIGHTS Writing an Interpretation Turn to the Constitution on pages 82–103 of the textbook. Work with a group of classmates to discuss the meanings of Article 4 (Relations Among States) and Amendment 10 (Powers of States and People). Then restate these passages in more contemporary English.

CIVIL RIGHTS Writing an Editorial The day after Congress passed the Thirteenth Amendment, a New York newspaper ran an editorial in support of its passage. The editorial declared: "The adoption of this amendment is the most important step ever

taken by Congress." Complete this editorial. State facts and arguments to support your position. End by urging quick ratification of the amendment.

VOTING RIGHTS Charting Milestones Create and complete a chart entitled "Milestones in Voting Rights, 1776–1877." Column heads should include: date, event, importance to voting rights.

WOMEN AND POLITICAL POWER Making a Speech Imagine that it is 1880 and you are one of the few women delegates to either the Republican or Democratic national convention. Together with several of your classmates write a plank for your party's platform coming out in favor of women's suffrage. Then prepare and deliver a speech in which you present the party's position and defend it.

ECONOMIC OPPORTUNITY Holding a Panel Discussion French traveler Alexis de Toqueville made the following assessment of the United States in the early 1830s.

> *An American will build a house in which to pass his old age and sell it before the roof is on; he will plant a garden and rent it just as the trees are coming into bearing; . . . he will take up a profession and leave it, settle in one place and soon go off elsewhere with his changing desires.*

Organize a panel discussion of the passage.

SCIENCE AND TECHNOLOGY Designing an Ad Review the innovations described in the Thematic Review on page 196. Select one of these items and create an advertisement announcing its sale or use to the public.

Answer Key

Geography Skills 1

1. Mercator, Robinson, Goode's Interrupted, and Polar

2. On the Mercator projection Greenland and Antarctica appear much larger than they do on the Robinson projection.

3. Because it is cut into sections, Goode's Interrupted projection does not show a continuous view of the earth.

4. Because the world is shown on a grid of straight lines, an area that is directly north of another area on the earth, for instance, will appear directly above the area on the map.

Geography Skills 2

1. Europe, Africa, and Antarctica

2. 180°

3. South America

4. (Check students' locations)

Geography Skills 3

1. North America, South America, Africa, Europe, Asia, Australia, Antarctica

2. North of the equator

3. The Indian Ocean

4. The Mediterranean Sea

Geography Skills 4

1. The equator

2. The Eastern and Western Hemispheres

3. North America, Africa, Europe, and Asia

4. Asia and Antarctica

Geography Skills 5

1. Mountains, highlands, plateaus, and plains

2. Plateaus

3. The central region

4. Missouri River, east and Southeast; Colorado River, southwest and South; Rio Grand, south (Help students to realize that rivers flow from higher elevations to lower elevations, hence the usefulness of physical maps in determining the direction of rivers.)

Geography Skills 6

1. 200 miles; 400 kilometers

2. 300 miles; 500 kilometers

3. North

4. Southeast

Geography Skills 7

1. Gatun, Pedro Miguel, Miraflores

2. Gatun, Madden

3. Caribbean Sea and Bay of Panama (or Atlantic and Pacific Oceans)

4. Southeast

Geography Skills 8

1. Hot and dry, mild and dry, mild and wet, mountain region

2. The center and the southeastern region

3. The coast and the area just west of the mountain region

4. Both are mild, but Los Angeles is drier.

Chapter 1, Section 1
GUIDED READING

A. Possible answers:

1. Introduced such domesticated crops as corn, beans, and squash; built cities and ceremonial centers; created empires; conducted trade; built massive earthen structures, or mounds; crafted objects of metal and stone.

2. Created diverse cultures suitable to their environments; some harvested fish, others grew crops, and others combined hunting and agriculture; developed extensive trade networks; viewed the land as belonging to all and the natural world as filled with spiritual presences.

3. Created extensive kingdoms with sophisticated societies; built cities; had highly developed metalworking skills; traded with North Africa and Europe; some adopted the Islamic religion.

4. Created hierarchical society that supported wealthy monarchs and nobles; established powerful Roman Catholic Church which undertook Crusades; underwent Reformation;

developed corporations and joint-stock companies; created the Renaissance in arts and science; improved cartography and sailing technology.

B. Answers should be similar to the following:

Beringia land bridge: land connection between Asia and North America that existed until about 12,000 B.C. and across which the first human inhabitants traveled

Anasazi: ancient inhabitants of North America who mastered life in the arid Southwest

Pueblo: Native American group that lives in multi-story, adobe dwellings, builds kivas, and grows crops in desert conditions

Songhai: One of several powerful West African kingdoms from which Africans were brought to America as slaves

Reformation: A split in the Roman Catholic Church caused by those who wanted reform; created groups of Protestants some of whom came to North America seeking religious freedom

caravel: A sailing ship of advanced design that enabled sailors to navigate against the wind and brought early explorers to North America

Chapter 1, Section 2
GUIDED READING

A. Possible answers:

1. To find a direct water route to Asia; to convert Native Americans to Catholicism; and to find precious metals

2. Native American groups were decimated by disease; many Native Americans were enslaved; a massive trading exchange developed across the Atlantic; plantations and colonies developed in the Americas; missions were established

3. Greed for silver and gold; a desire to spread the Catholic religion; a desire to expand Spanish power

4. Superior weaponry and military supplies, such as firearms and horses; diseases

5. To advance the Catholic religion and to protect Spain's holdings from

other European nations

6. The European influence spread into present-day California, Texas, and New Mexico; some Native Americans were converted to Catholicism; some Native Americans, notably the Pueblo in New Mexico, resisted

B. Answers should be similar to the following:

conquistadors: Armed Spanish explorers who came to the Americas after Columbus

Hernán Cortés: Conquistador who conquered the Aztecs

mestizo: Person of mixed Spanish and Native American heritage

encomienda: Brutal system of organizing Native Americans to provide labor for the Spanish conquerors

Columbian Exchange: Worldwide trade in farm products and livestock among Europe, Africa, and the Americas

Taino: The first group of Native Americans encountered by Columbus, on Hispaniola

Popé: Pueblo religious leader who led a well-organized rebellion against Spanish missionaries in New Mexico in 1680

Chapter 1, Section 3
GUIDED READING

A. Possible answers:

1. English settlers poorly prepared for colonial life; indentured servants looking for a new life; Africans brought as slaves in 1619

2. Founder John Smith was charismatic, ambitious, and skilled in diplomacy and military arts.

3. Settlers wanted to strike it rich in the New World; Smith wanted to make money for his investors; indentured servants wanted passage and temporary support.

4. The Powhatan helped the new colonists at first but conflict developed as settlers moved onto more and more land; Indian rebellion died out as English population grew.

5. Puritans from England, mostly families

6. John Winthrop, Massachusetts Bay

Company

7. The Puritans wanted to escape religious persecution, political repression, and poor economic conditions in England.

8. Native Americans were very helpful to the colonists at the beginning; resentment grew with the spread of European diseases and the loss of land to settlers; disputes arose about land ownership and religion.

9. Dutch West India Company; Dutch, Swedish, Finnish; people of many religions

10. To expand the thriving fur trade and build a colony

11. Both groups had motivation for cooperation in the fur trade.

12. In 1644, England took over the colony from the Dutch without a fight, renaming it New York.

13. English Quakers

14. William Penn, Society of Friends

15. To establish a good and fair society embodying their ideals of equality, cooperation, and religious tolerance

16. Penn approached the Delaware with respect and friendship, bought land rather than simply taking it, and encouraged fair treatment of Native Americans.

Chapter 1, Section 4
GUIDED READING

A. Possible answers:

Northern Colonies

• produced several cash crops per farm;

• developed many thriving commercial industries;

• developed a powerful merchant class;

• had numerous cities;

• had more ethnic, religious, and national groups represented among their populations

Southern Colonies

• produced single crops of rice, indigo, or tobacco;

• had an economy based primarily on farming;

• relied more heavily on slave labor;

• had fewer merchants;

• had few major cities and only one important port, Charles Town;

• had a less diverse population

B. Possible answers:

1. Enlightenment: intellectual movement

   Great Awakening: religious movement

2. Enlightenment: Benjamin Franklin, Thomas Jefferson

   Great Awakening: Jonathan Edwards, George Whitefield

3. Enlightenment: The natural world is governed not by miracles or chance, but by fixed mathematical laws; truth can be found by using reason, observation, and experimentation; individuals have natural rights.

   Great Awakening: People should return to Puritan values and rededicate themselves to God; people need salvation; people can experience God directly; education is important; individuals can question authority.

4. Enlightenment: To use experimentation and observation as tools to make discoveries about the natural world; to rely on reason; to read and learn; to question traditional authority, including that of the British monarchy

   Great Awakening: To rededicate themselves to God; to join organized churches; to found colleges for training ministers; to read the Bible; to question traditional authority

Chapter 1
BUILDING VOCABULARY

A.

1. i	6. j
2. f	7. a
3. e	8. g
4. b	9. d
5. c	10. h

B.

1. Christianity

2. Renaissance

3. Columbian Exchange

4. John Winthrop

5. Proclamation of 1763

C. Answers will vary; accept reasonable responses.

Chapter 1, Section 1
SKILLBUILDER PRACTICE

1. Plains. They are in the middle of the orange color, identified as Plains on the key.

2. Any two of the following: Tuscarora, Creek, Seminole, Powhatan, Susquehanna, Delaware Wampanoag, Pequot, Narragansett Iroquois

3. Yurok, Hupa, Kato, Kashaya Pomo, Chumash

4. Roughly 1700 miles, although some distances will be slightly longer or shorter depending on how precise students' measurements are. Most students will probably mark off the distance on a piece of paper and measure that distance against the scale. Some students might place a piece of string along the line and then measure the string against the scale.

5. Any three of the following: Haida, Nootka, Kwakiutl, Blackfoot, Cree, Chippewa, Ottawa, Algonquin, Huichol, Aztec, Maya, Taino, Apache

6. About 700 miles, west to the Pacific Ocean

7. The Chinook would have had to travel southeast a little more than 1000 miles to get to Arapaho country if they went in a straight line. Students may think it is unlikely that the Chinook would have traveled there because the way would have been through two mountain ranges and other rough terrain, and no major trade routes went that way. Also, the Chinook had a coastal way of life and would have had no reason to travel to the Plains.

Chapter 1, Section 2
SKILLBUILDER PRACTICE

1. Students answers will vary.

2. Students answers will vary.

Chapter 1, Section 4
SKILLBUILDER PRACTICE

Possible entries in Venn diagram:

Cliveden House: Differences—spacious home, surrounded by trees, numerous windows, private, houses appear spread out; Elfreth's Alley—small homes, no trees, few windows, crowded conditions; little privacy; Similarities—both appear made of brick; use of shutters.

1. Some students may say the size of the homes is the most significant difference, while others may say the cramped and crowded condition of the homes in Elfreth's Alley compared to the feeling of isolation and privacy of the Cliveden Home.

2. Most students will say that the scene in Elfreth's Alley shows the more accurate depiction of urban life in the colonies because most colonists in the cities belonged to either the lower or middle class and thus lived in homes and along streets similar to the one shown here.

3. Possible sources: diaries, some history books, eyewitness accounts, engravings and paintings

Chapter 1, Section 1
RETEACHING ACTIVITY

1. F—The Aztec settled in the valley of Mexico during the 1200s and developed a thriving and sophisticated civilization.

2. T

3. F—By the 1400s, the kingdoms of Africa had developed trading relationships with Europe and Asia.

4. T

5. F—The Crusades was a military expedition to reclaim the Holy Land around Jerusalem for Christians.

6. F—The four major nations that emerged in Europe during the 1400s were Portugal, Spain, France, and England.

7. T

8. F—The Portuguese led the way for European exploration by first rounding the southern tip of Africa and later reaching India.

Chapter 1, Section 2
RETEACHING ACTIVITY

A.

1. H	5. A
2. D	6. F
3. B	7. E
4. C	8. G

B.

1. Netherlands, England

2. France

3. France

4. England

5. Spain

6. France

Chapter 1, Section 3
RETEACHING ACTIVITY

1. c	5. c
2. a	6. a
3. b	7. b
4. a	8. c

Chapter 1, Section 4
RETEACHING ACTIVITY

Possible Answers

I.

A. Large farms specialize in raising a single cash crop, such as tobacco, rice, and indigo

B. Society somewhat diverse with many German immigrants and Scots and Scots-Irish

C. Dependence on agriculture led to the growth of slavery

II.

A. Farms were smaller and grew a diversity of crops rather than one cash crop

B. Growth of trade led to rise of cities and a powerful merchant class

C. Highly diverse society with immigrants from numerous European countries

III.

A. Suggested that people could use logic and science—rather than church teachings—to arrive at the truth

B. Led colonists to reason that people are born with natural rights that governments must respect

IV.

A. Challenged the authority of established churches

B. Prompted colonists to worship more independently and form new denominations

V.

A. War between England and France over colonial dominance of North America

B. Colonists and British join forces to defeat the French and their Native American allies

C. Victory provides England with control over entire eastern half of North America

Chapter 1, Section 4
GEOGRAPHY APPLICATION

Responses may vary on the inferential questions. Sample responses are given for those.

1. The path of the trade route resembles a triangle.

2. The transporting of Africans across the Atlantic Ocean as slaves

3. The West Indies and the British Colonies; some slaves were kept in the West Indies to help in the harvesting of sugar cane for the last "leg" of the triangle route.

4. New England

5. The Southern Colonies

6. It shrank. The economies of New England and the middle colonies, depending less on agriculture, did not seek vast numbers of slave workers. Slavery never caught on in these areas as it did in the South.

7. Plantations were expanding and needed more workers. This spurred the growth of the slave trade and increased the percentage of Africans in the Southern colonies.

Chapter 1, Section 2
OUTLINE MAP

1. Ponce de León

2. Coronado; nearly 2,000 miles

3. De Soto

4. Possible response: west from the Gulf of Mexico through present-day Texas, across to northern Mexico, south along the west coast of Mexico, then eastward toward Tenochtitlán

5. Cortés, Ponce de León, Cabrillo

6. De Soto and Cortés

7. a. Florida, Georgia, South Carolina, North Carolina, Tennessee, Alabama, Mississippi, Arkansas, Louisiana

b. Arizona, New Mexico, Texas, Oklahoma, Kansas

Chapter 1, Section 1
PRIMARY SOURCE

The Iroquois Constitution

1. Possible meanings for the tree: union with nature, organic connection among nations, permanence and stability, protection and security, goodness

2. Possible advantages: an end to inter-tribal warfare; a stronger coalition against enemies, including the coming tide of Europeans; a fair system of government and law. Possible disadvantage: the league may have sparked jealously and envy among other groups and so caused conflict.

3. Possible similarities: the division of power between two branches of government; the stress on union; the clear organization of the government; the stress on a common defense. Possible differences: the Iroquois constitution has more emphasis on nature and obedience to the law; the U.S. Constitution has more emphasis on numbers, qualifications, roles, and elections.

Chapter 1, Section 2
PRIMARY SOURCE

The Journal of Christopher Columbus

1. Students may be impressed by any of the following: the actions and

feelings expressed by all parties at the historic meeting; the description of the Taino; Columbus's observations and thoughts about the Taino; the character of Columbus as revealed in his observations and thoughts.

2. Gold is Columbus's main interest because the purpose of the voyage is to gain more wealth for Spain.

3. Possible response: Columbus reveals a superior attitude toward the Taino, although he seems to be fair and at times respectful in his descriptions. He basically considers them servants. He also assumes that they cannot talk, possibly because they do not talk to him.

Chapter 1, Section 3
PRIMARY SOURCE

Travels and Works of Captain John Smith
Possible responses:

1. Smith was treated with a mixture of curiosity, respect, and animosity. On the one hand, the Powhatan people captured him and threatened to kill him. On the other hand, they dressed in their finest clothing and held a feast to honor him. Finally, they treated him as a bargaining chip, returning him to Jamestown in exchange for guns, a millstone, and other presents.

2. According to Smith, his life was spared because Pocahontas intervened and because Chief Powhatan realized that Smith was more useful to him alive than dead.

3. Students may point out that the Powhatan people and the English had cultural differences, including language barriers, religious beliefs, and traditions. They may also mention that the English neither respected nor understood the Powhatan way of life, as illustrated by Smith's condescending references to them as savages and barbarians.

Chapter 1, Section 4
PRIMARY SOURCE

The Autobiography

1. Students' oral reports will vary. They may research the Franklin stove, bifocals, the lightning rod, or

Franklin's groundbreaking studies of electricity and the movement of the Gulf Stream in the Atlantic Ocean.

2. Paragraphs will vary. Students may note that the influence of the Enlightenment is evident in Franklin's reliance on experimentation, observation, and reason to discover the principles and natural laws that govern the world.

Chapter 1, Section 2
LITERATURE SELECTION

The Memoirs of Christopher Columbus

1. Suggest that students read the primary source from Columbus's journal to get a complete picture of the event. Informally assess skits on the accuracy of detail and actions and on the depth of imaginative expression.

2. Encourage students to display their sketches in the classroom and then compare their illustrated versions of the first encounter. You may prefer to have students work together as a class to create a mural based on descriptive details that they glean from this excerpt.

Chapter 1, Section 3
AMERICAN LIVES

John Winthrop
Possible responses:

1. By "city upon a hill," Winthrop meant that the colony would be a model for other settlements and would serve God and society with the priority of a community set aside for that purpose.

2. Winthrop left because the economic and political situation in England had worsened and he believed in the need to have a separate church to reform it.

3. Winthrop rejected democracy because he had little faith in common people to govern themselves and because there was no such thing in the Bible, which formed the basis of his political beliefs.

Chapter 1, Section 4
AMERICAN LIVES

Olaudah Equiano
Possible responses:

1. By showing the virtues of Africans—hard work, modest manners, and lack of alcohol—Equiano hoped to persuade English readers that these people should not be taken as slaves.

2. The cruel treatment of the Middle Passage contrasts with the virtuous life in Africa and shows the violation of Christian principles.

3. Equiano used economic arguments against the slave trade to convince those who would not be persuaded by the moral reasons.

Chapter 2, Section 1
GUIDED READING

A. Possible answers:

1. a. The British Parliament passed the act to finance debts.

   b. Colonists responded to the act by organizing the Sons of Liberty; demonstrating and protesting and boycotting British goods.

   c. Parliament responded to the colonists by repealing the Stamp Act.

2. a. Parliament passed the act to increase revenues from the colonies.

   b. Colonists responded to the act by demonstrating and protesting; boycotting British goods.

   c. Parliament responded to the colonists by enforcing the act; stationing troops in Boston; then repealing the act.

3. a. Parliament passed the act in order to save the East India Company from bankruptcy.

   b. Colonists responded to the act by dumping 15,000 pounds of the East India Company's tea into the waters of Boston harbor, holding the Boston Tea Party.

   c. Parliament responded to the colonists by passing the Intolerable Acts.

4. a. Parliament passed the acts to

punish the colonists for the Boston Tea Party; to tighten control over Massachusetts.

   b. Colonists responded to the acts by holding the First Continental Congress; pulling together to support the protests in Massachusetts; stepping up military preparations.

   c. Parliament responded to the colonists by marching troops to Concord to seize illegal weapons and by engaging the colonists in battle.

B. Answers will vary widely depending upon the specifics noted.

Chapter 2, Section 2
GUIDED READING

A. Possible answers:

1. Winners: The British

   Reasons: Their better-trained and better-equipped forces overwhelmed the Continentals.

   Results: The British captured New York.

2. Winners: The Americans

   Reasons: They took the overconfident Germans by surprise.

   Results: The Americans took Trenton; American morale rose.

3. Winners: The Americans

   Reasons: Britain's General Burgoyne underestimated the difficulties of fulfilling his plan of attack; British forces failed to aid Burgoyne's. The Continentals saw that they could beat the British; British confidence was damaged; France was convinced to support the Americans openly.

4. Winners: The Americans

   Reasons: American and French armies joined forces with French fleets to attack Cornwallis at Yorktown; French and American troops surrounded the British on the Yorktown peninsula and bombarded them day and night.

   Results: The British surrendered; peace talks that began in Paris in 1782 resulted in the Treaty of Paris; treaty confirmed U.S. independence.

B. Possible answers:

1. Remaining clothed; keeping fed; staying warm and healthy; having to

provide their own housing; keeping their spirits up

2. Financing the war; battling inflation; equipping the army; negotiating with France

3. Managing farms, businesses, families, and households; caring for soldiers in the field

C. Answers will vary widely depending upon the specifics noted.

Chapter 2, Section 3
GUIDED READING

A. Possible answers:

1. Virginia Plan: two houses, a lower and an upper house

2. New Jersey Plan: a single house

3. Each state's population

4. One vote per state

5. It proposed a bicameral Congress, giving each state equal representation in the Senate and representation based on population in the House of Representatives.

6. People, other than slaves

7. People, including slaves

8. It proposed that three-fifths of a state's slaves be counted for representation.

B. Answers will vary widely depending on the specifics noted.

Chapter 2, Section 4
GUIDED READING

A. Possible answers:

1. Set up the federal court system; established federal circuit and district courts; allowed state court decisions involving the federal Constitution to be appealed to a federal court

2. State, headed by Thomas Jefferson; War, headed by Henry Knox; and Treasury, headed by Alexander Hamilton

3. Distrusted centralized power; trusted the common people

4. Favored centralized power; distrusted the common people

5. Believed it was unconstitutional

6. Believed it would help to organize and stabilize the nation's finances; believed it would tie wealthy investors to the nation's success

7. Democratic-Republican

8. Federalist

9. Federalist support-Northerners; Democratic-Republican support-Southerners

B. Answers will vary widely depending upon the specifics noted.

Chapter 2
BUILDING VOCABULARY

A.

1. b
2. c
3. a
4. d
5. a

B.

1. d
2. h
3. f
4. j
5. g
6. e
7. b
8. a
9. c
10. i

C. Answers will vary; accept reasonable responses

Chapter 2 , Section 2
SKILLBUILDER PRACTICE

Responses will vary; possibilities follow:

2. EFFECT/CAUSE: France wants to challenge Britain to regain lost American colonies.

5. EFFECT/CAUSE: French soldiers join American soldiers.

8. EFFECT: American and French forces defeat the British at the Battle of Yorktown.

Chapter 2, Section 3
SKILLBUILDER PRACTICE

1. Great Britain

2. Possible Answer: It meant that the troops would have to wait a long time for ammunition and supplies.

3. Possible Answer: It would allow them to escape trouble more easily or hide out, as well as to lead the British into traps.

4. Possible Answer: Most students will say the British because they had the stronger and better-equipped army, while the colonists had an untrained army, a weak navy, and a constant shortage of supplies and ammunition.

Chapter 2, Section 4
SKILLBUILDER PRACTICE

Any five of the following possibilities:

Category

1. Place of birth
2. Youth
3. College
4. Government service
5. Military action in Revolutionary War

Jefferson

1. Virginia
2. life of a country boy
3. College of William and Mary
4. Second Continental Congress, drafted Declaration of Independence, President
5. none

Hamilton

1. West Indies
2. worked for trading company
3. King's College
4. Congress of the Confederation, Secretary of Treasury
5. captain

Chapter 2, Section 1
RETEACHING ACTIVITY

1. It was the first tax that directed the colonies directly; previous taxes had been indirect, involving duties on imports.

2. The Boston Tea Party; The acts shut down Boston harbor and forced the colonists to house British soldiers.

3. May 1775; it debated independence, recognized the colonial militia as the Continental Army, and appointed George Washington as commander.

4. He rejected the petition, declared the colonists to be in rebellion, and urged Parliament to order a naval blockade of the American coast.

5. Independence would allow Americans to trade more freely and would give the colonists the chance to start a new society with greater social equality and economic opportunity.

6. A government's power came from the consent of the governed, and thus the people could abolish a government that threatened their basic rights.

Chapter 2, Section 2
RETEACHING ACTIVITY

A.

1. 5	5. 4
2. 6	6. 3
3. 1	7. 2
4. 8	8. 7

B.

1. F—Those colonists who supported independence were know as Patriots.

2. T

3. F—The Continental Army spent the winter of 1777-1778 in harsh conditions at Valley Forge.

4. T

5. F—Many African Americans remained enslaved and women remained second-class citizens with few rights.

Chapter 2, Section 3
RETEACHING ACTIVITY

Large state v. small state: Conflict—large states wanted two-house legislature with representation in both houses based on a state's population; small states wanted single-house legislature with equal representation among states; Compromise—Great Compromise created a two-house legislature with equal representation in the Senate and representation in the House of Representatives based on a state's population

North v. South: Conflict—Southern states wanted to include their slave populations in determining representation for the House of Representatives; Northern states, which had small slave populations, opposed this idea; Compromise—Three-Fifths Compromise, which called for three-fifths of a state's slave population to be counted for the purposes of representation

Ratification: Conflict—Federalists favored the balance of power established by the Constitution and supported its ratification; Antifederalists believed that the Constitution granted too much power to the central government and thus opposed its ratification; Compromise—The Federalists promised to include in the Constitution a Bill of Rights to protect citizens' basic rights and freedoms

Chapter 2, Section 4
RETEACHING ACTIVITY

1. b

2. c

3. a

4. d

5. a

6. b

Chapter 2, Section 2
GEOGRAPHY APPLICATION

Responses may vary on the inferential questions. Sample responses are given for those.

1. Cornwallis wanted it to be possible to receive supplies and reinforcements by ship from New York and aid from British naval forces in the Atlantic Ocean.

2. French ships had set up a blockade, preventing British ships from entering or leaving the Yorktown area; the York River had no outlet to the Atlantic.

3. American lines of defense and

troops; French troops.

4. Retreat across the York River appears the only means of escape. With that route cut off and boats disabled by the storm, Cornwallis's position was hopeless.

5. Yorktown is located on a peninsula. A French fleet blocked escape to and reinforcements from the east. American and French troops blocked escape to the south and west. Cornwallis was trapped, and bad weather prevented his only means of retreat across the York River.

6. The British presence in North America began and ended in almost the same spot on the continent—Jamestown and Yorktown.

Chapter 2, Section 2
PRIMARY SOURCE

The Boston Tea Party

1. Possible causes: colonists opposed Tea Act; colonists refused to withdraw their opposition to the landing of the tea; Governor Hutchinson failed to meet with a committee of colonists to discuss the situation.

   Possible effects: the colonists decided to take drastic measures against the British; three parties of colonists boarded the ships and disposed of the tea; some Bostonians tried to steal tea.

2. Informally assess students on their participation in the planning and performing of their reenactment. You may want to videotape their performance to share with other history classes.

3. Informally assess students on the degree of skill and amount of thought that went into their alternative protests.

Chapter 2, Section 2
PRIMARY SOURCE

Political Cartoon

1. Students' research should reveal that Lord Shelburne was thought by some to have abandoned the American empire and ignored the Loyalists' pleas for justice.

2. Charts will vary. Challenges might include harassment, tarring and feathering, loss of property, return to England, isolation, exile to Canada and the Caribbean.

Chapter 2, Section 2
PRIMARY SOURCE

Valley Forge Diary

1. Informally assess students' sketches to make sure they have incorporated details from the diary entries.

2. Possible responses:

   Sights: butcher's white buttons

   Sounds: cry of "No meat!", crow and owl imitations

   Tastes: fire cake, mutton, grog

   Smells: smoke

   Touch: smoke, cold

Chapter 2, Section 3
PRIMARY SOURCE

The U.S. Constitution, First Draft

Possible responses:

1. Major differences: the Preamble in final copy is much more detailed and concrete; the concept of "the United States of America" is assumed rather than stated; the articles in the final copy are much longer, more explicit, and more detailed than in the first draft.

2. The union of the country and the power of the federal government are emphasized over the existence of the individual states and their governments. It was important to declare this union in the Constitution to ensure that the federal government would always remain stronger than the state governments.

Chapter 2, Section 3
LITERATURE SELECTION

Legacy

1. Simon and Jared Starr are the only fictional characters.

2. You may want to have students research other delegates who are not mentioned in this excerpt. Encourage the class to add illustrations to make their biographical portraits come to life.

Chapter 2, Section 2
AMERICAN LIVES

Haym Salomon

Possible responses:

1. The principles of equality and freedom of religion would appeal to Jewish people, who often suffered persecution in Europe.

2. Salomon helped with finances. He raised money by selling bonds to the Dutch and French at a tiny percentage of commission, and he handled the paying of French soldiers. He also loaned money to Madison, Jefferson, and others.

3. In the face of prejudice, Salomon felt the need to defend the role of Jewish people in the Revolution.

Chapter 2, Section 3
AMERICAN LIVES

Patrick Henry

Possible responses:

1. In the Continental Congress, he declared that identity as an American was more important than that as a Virginian. In the debate over the Constitution, he wanted to downplay national power.

2. He dispatched George Rogers Clark to help secure Virginia's claims to western lands and opposed the Constitution because it lessened Virginia's power.

3. The Bill of Rights is the keystone of U.S. democracy, providing the absolute protection of the rights of the individual.

The Living Constitution, Preamble and Article 1
GUIDED READING

Answers:

1. Yes	2.2	7. No	7.3
2. No	3.3	8. No	9.3
3. Yes	3.4	9. No	10.2
4. No	6.1	10. Yes	5.1
5. No	6.2	11. No	7.2
6. Yes	5.2	12. Yes	10.3

The Living Constitution, Articles 2 and 3
GUIDED READING

Answers: Article 2

1. Yes	6. Yes
2. Yes	7. Yes
3. No	8. Yes
4. No	9. Yes
5. No	10. No

Article 3

11. No	14. No
12. No	15. Yes
13. Yes	16. No

The Living Constitution, Articles 4–7
GUIDED READING

Answers: Article 4

1. Yes	4.1	2. No	4.2.2
3. Yes	4.3.1	4. No	4.4

Article 5

5. Congress   5

6. ¾ (or today, 38)   5

Article 6

7. No	6.2	8. No	6.3
9. No	6.3	

Article 7

10. 9   7   11. 1787   7

The Living Constitution, The Amendments
GUIDED READING

1. criticize the government

2. armed militias

3. house

4. good reason

5. fair payment

6. people accused of crimes

7 jury

8. unfair or cruel

9. are not

10. states or the people

11. state

12. the person they choose for each office

13. United States

14. equal protection under the law

15. race

16. an income

17. U.S. senators

18. prohibition

19. sex

20. shortens

21. 18

22. number

23. presidential

24. voting

25. vice president

26. citizens

27. members of Congress

The Living Constitution
BUILDING VOCABULARY

A.

1. preamble

2. legislative

3. electoral college

4. Judicial review

5. amendments

B

1. d

2. e

3. f

4. a

5. c

6. b

C. Answers will vary; accept reasonable responses.

The Living Constitution
SKILLBUILDER PRACTICE

Responses will vary but should include the important points of the amendment, such as the following:

1. safe, free from the risk of loss

2. personal belongings

3. the act of forcibly taking possession of something

4. a legal document authorizing an

officer to search a place or person, to take possession of someone's things, or to arrest a person

5. be issued or approved

6. reasonable grounds for believing something

7. a solemn statement of facts, like an oath or vow

8. People have a right to be protected from others searching them or their property or taking their belongings without good reasons.

9. Search warrants and warrants for arrest can't be issued without good reason supported by an oath or a written statement describing in detail the property to be searched, the person to be arrested, or the belongings to be taken.

The Living Constitution
RETEACHING ACTIVITIES

Article 1

1. House of Representatives; Senate

2. revenue; money; commerce

3. elastic

4. president

5. impeachment

6. two-thirds

7. two; six

Articles 2 & 3

1. T

2. F—The vice-president is the first in line to succeed the president should he or she become unable to perform the duties of the office.

3. F—The president may make treaties with foreign nations with the advice and consent of the Senate.

4. T

5. T

6. F—Justices to the Supreme Court are appointed by the president.

Articles 4-7

1. The Constitution guarantees each state protection against domestic violence; president can order forces to maintain order.

2. The person must be returned to the first state upon the state's demand.

3. two-thirds of each house of Congress, or by a convention called by two-thirds of the state legislatures

4. three-fourths of the state legislatures, or by three-fourths of special conventions held in each state

5. religious

6. nine

7. September 17, 1787

The Amendments

1. c

2. b

3. c

4. d

5. d

6. a

7. b

8. b

The Living Constitution
GEOGRAPHY APPLICATION

Responses may vary on the inferential questions. Sample responses are given for those.

1. It was a compromise between those who wanted Congress to elect the president and those who wanted the people to elect the chief executive.

2. It is equal to a state's total members in the House and Senate.

3. Some of the delegates either mistrusted the average American citizen's motives or had a low opinion of his ability to cast an informed vote.

4. Alaska, Delaware, North Dakota, South Dakota, Vermont, Wyoming, and the District of Columbia; 3

5. Citizens vote for candidates, who actually represent a group of electors in their states. The winning group of electors then cast votes directly for a presidential candidate.

6. Though losing the overall popular vote, a candidate can manage to become president by winning, however slightly, in many or most of the largest of the states and capturing all

their high number of electoral votes.

7. Citizens expect the "winner" of the popular vote to be the president and can be shocked and suspicious if the electoral vote that comes later proves to have a different outcome.

The Living Constitution
AMERICAN LIVES

James Madison

Possible responses:

1. A shy person like Madison is unlikely to succeed in politics now. Modern campaigns placed too many demands on campaigners for speaking and public appearances.

2. To promote religious freedom, Madison won approval of a call for free exercise of religion and disestablished the Anglican Church in Virginia. Also, the First Amendment, which he wrote, guarantees religious freedom.

3. Madison wrote the Bill of Rights, which is attached to the Constitution and without which the Constitution probably could not have been adopted.

The Living Constitution
AMERICAN LIVES

Thurgood Marshall

Possible responses:

1. In arguing, and winning, the *Brown* case, among others, Marshall had already made a significant impact on history.

2. The *Brown* decision was based on the Fourteenth and Fifteenth Amendments, which were not part of the original Constitution.

3. Marshall's last dissent asserts the need to use the Constitution to protect "the powerless," which was a major concern of his.

Chapter 3, Section 1
GUIDED READING

A. Possible answers:

1. Reduced the size of government and military; cut costs; eliminated internal taxes; reduced influence of the national bank

2. Jefferson ushered in the beginning of Southern dominance of national politics, which weakened the influence of the Federalists.

3. It prompted passage of the Twelfth Amendment, which called for electors to cast separate ballots for president and vice-president.

4. Affirmed the principle of judicial review (the ability of the Supreme Court to declare an act of Congress unconstitutional)

5. Doubled the size of U.S. territory; expanded the power of the presidency and the central government

6. Brought back valuable information about the West; showed that cross-country travel was possible; opened the way for settlement of the West

B. Answers will vary depending on the specifics noted.

C. Answers will vary depending on the specifics noted.

Chapter 3, Section 2
GUIDED READING

A. Possible answers:

1. As speaker of the house, Henry Clay had great influence in Congress. Clay disliked and distrusted Jackson. Clay and the rest of Congress elected Adams to be president.

2. The federal government would provide funds to negotiate treaties that would force Native Americans to move west.

3. Calhoun's theory held that the U.S. Constitution was based on a compact among the sovereign states. Since the states never relinquished their sovereignty, each state retained the right to determine whether acts of Congress were constitutional. If a state decided an act was unconstitutional, it could nullify the act within its borders.

4. More Americans became involved in the political process. Also, the West was playing an increasing role in national politics.

5. Many of the pet banks that accepted federal deposits were wildcat banks that failed when people tried to redeem their currency for gold or silver.

B. Answers will vary depending upon the specifics noted.

Chapter 3, Section 3
GUIDED READING

A. Possible answers:

1. Texas: empresarios; settlers

   Oregon: settlers; missionaries; farmers

   Utah: Mormon settlers

2. Texas: to collect land grants

   Oregon: to farm; to convert Native Americans to Christianity

   Utah: to avoid religious persecution

3. Texas: Text does not say, but students might infer that they traveled with horses and wagons on a route similar to the Butterfield route.

   Oregon: Oregon Trail; walked; wagon trains

   Utah: Oregon Trail; walked; wagon trains

4. Causes: U.S. victory in the War with Mexico

   Results: United States gains territory, including California; United States pays Mexico for Texas.

B. Austin and Houston were central characters in the early history of Texas, and the massacre at the Alamo was the turning point in the Texas Revolution.

C. Possible answers:

   Manifest destiny: the belief that America was destined to expand to the Pacific Ocean

   Oregon Trail: trail that settlers followed to the Oregon territory

   Republic of California: name given to the nation established by California rebels after U.S. troops expelled the Mexican army from the region

Chapter 3, Section 4
GUIDED READING

1. Provided investment capital to create new companies and industries that boosted U.S. industrial output

2. Improved communication; allowed businesspersons to stay in contact; helped trains move more efficiently

and safely; linked regions of the country

3. Improved transportation; reduced travel time for goods and people, allowing agricultural and industrial expansion; decreased freight charges

4. Decreased travel time for goods and people; linked regions of the country

5. Opened more efficient trade routes; decreased freight charges; linked regions

6. Made farming more efficient; allowed farmers to shift from subsistence farming to growing cash crops

7. Brought workers into factory to make goods; introduced workers to industrial work discipline; allowed unskilled workers to replace skilled artisans

8. Offered workers a chance to expand their power in the workplace by organizing efforts to improve pay and working conditions

9. Declared that workers had the legal right to organize to protect their rights

10. Created many jobs; produced goods efficiently; created new markets; produced new goods for use in other sectors of the economy (agriculture, transportation)

B. Answers will vary depending on the specifics noted.

Chapter 3, Section 5
GUIDED READING

A. Possible answers:

1. Strengthening religious faith; opposing slavery; offered education and social services

2. Immediate abolition of slavery

3. Equality for women; increasing women's rights; encouraging women to participate in reform movements; woman suffrage

4. Truth found in nature, intuition, and imagination; the dignity of the individual

5. William Lloyd Garrison and the founding of *The Liberator;* Frederick Douglass and the founding of the *North Star;* Nat Turner's

rebellion; Elizabeth Cady Stanton; Sojourner Truth; the World's Anti-Slavery Convention

6. As a promise of freedom

7. Although only a small percentage of women received much formal education, the opportunities for women increased, offering more women access to new areas of study than were previously available.

B. Answers will vary depending upon the specifics noted.

Chapter 3
BUILDING VOCABULARY

A.

1. f	6. i
2. j	7. d
3. h	8. g
4. c	9. e
5. a	10. b

B.

1. Frederick Douglass

2. market revolution

3. Manifest destiny

4. Missouri Compromise

5. Jeffersonian republicanism

C.

Answers will vary; accept reasonable responses

Chapter 3, Section 1
SKILLBUILDER PRACTICE

1. To be wise and frugal; to restrain people from injuring one another; to leave people free to follow their own interests; not to overtax people

2. He probably feels that the government is likely to overtax and overspend. This is apparent from his cautions against the government interfering in people's lives and taking "from the mouth of labor the bread that it has earned," that is, taxing income.

3. He appears to feel that the government does not have a right to tax income.

4. He would most likely decrease the

power of government, at least in the areas of taxation and regulation.

5. Jefferson tried to shrink the government and cut costs. He cut the size of the army and limited the size of the navy. He lowered government expenses and reduced taxes.

Chapter 3, Section 2
SKILLBUILDER PRACTICE

1. Example 1 **does** illustrate nationalism because it shows how people were patriotic and proud of the accomplishments of their fellow Americans, and they felt a group identity as Americans. The people saw the frontiersmen at the Battle of New Orleans as heroes and refused to think that anything but American skill was responsible for the victory.

2. Example 2 **does not** illustrate nationalism because it describes conflicts and distrust among different segments of the American population. The people involved are thinking about the interests of their own regions or groups instead of the interests of the nation as a whole.

Chapter 3, Section 3
SKILLBUILDER PRACTICE

Students' responses will vary, but they will probably resemble the following:

1. Assumption: The United States has a right to step in and control another country as it chooses.

circled: implied, bias

2. Assumption: Mexico is inferior to the United States; Mexicans are incapable of developing their country on their own.

circled: states directly, bias

Chapter 3, Section 5
SKILLBUILDER PRACTICE

Any three of the following possibilities:

1. Problem: Small gains here and there, such as the right to own property, satisfied many women and they didn't feel the need to fight for more progress.

Directly stated

Clues: "One reason for the slow

progress. . . . "

2. Problem: The close association of women's rights with the abolition movement slowed down its progress. The portion of the public that was against abolition did not want to support a cause related to abolition.

Directly stated

Clues: "Much of the general public scorned reform in both areas."

3. Problem: Women could work for the causes of temperance or education reform, and those causes took energy away from the struggle for women's rights.

Directly stated

Clues: "The campaign for full equality for women also suffered as energy and attention were directed at temperance educational reforms."

4. Problem: The movement for equality for women went against the popular ideal of the woman taking care of her home.

Implied

Clues: ". . . they could easily work for temperance and educational reforms and still be seen as taking care of their families, rather than as going against the popular ideal of women's place being in the home."

Chapter 3, Section 1
RETEACHING ACTIVITY

1. The House of Representatives had to decide the election after Jefferson and his running mate received the same number of votes. To avoid such a situation again, Congress passed the Twelfth Amendment, which called for electors to cast separate ballots for president and vice-president.

2. The ability of the Supreme Court to declare a law unconstitutional.

3. It more than doubled the size of the nation and provided the country with new resources and lands to explore.

4. It led to the end of the Federalist Party; it encouraged the growth of American industries; it confirmed the status of the United States as a free and independent nation.

5. He fixed the northern U.S. border

at the 49th parallel from Michigan to the Rocky Mountains; he reached an agreement with Britain to jointly occupy the Oregon Territory; he convinced Spain to give Florida to the United States.

6. European powers were not to interfere with affairs in the Western Hemisphere, while the U.S. would not interfere in European matters.

Chapter 3, Section 2
RETEACHING ACTIVITY

A.

1. F—Industry first took hold in New England because agriculture there was not highly profitable and many citizens were ready to embrace new forms of manufacturing.

2. T

3. F—The American System consisted of establishing a protective tariff, rechartering the national bank, and sponsoring internal improvements

4. T

B.

Nullification Crisis—opposed states' rights and nullification, urged Congress to pass the Force Bill to allow president to use the military to enforce federal law; National Bank—opposed national bank, killed the bank by withdrawing all federal deposits and placing them in state banks; Indian Removal—supported removal of Indians, defied Supreme Court and ordered U.S. troops to remove Indians.

Chapter 3, Section 3
RETEACHING ACTIVITY

A.

1. 5	5. 7
2. 4	6. 3
3. 8	7. 6
4. 2	8. 1

B.

1. slavery

2. War for Texas Independence

3. Horace Greeley

4. Land

5. New Mexico and California

Chapter 3, Section 4
RETEACHING ACTIVITY

1. c

2. a

3. b

4. d

5. c

6. a

Chapter 3, Section 5
RETEACHING ACTIVITY

Abolition—William Lloyd Garrison establishes *The Liberator* to promote the immediate end of slavery; Frederick Douglass speaks out against slavery and forms his own anti-slavery newspaper; Sojourner Truth speaks out against slavery; women abolitionists raise money, distribute literature, and work to send anti-slavery petitions to Congress; Anti-Slavery Convention convenes in 1840. Women's Issues—reformers improve educational opportunities for women by establishing women's colleges and other institutions; Elizabeth Cady Stanton and Lucretia Mott organize Seneca Falls Convention to demand greater rights for women, including the right to vote.

Possible Answer: Some students might say that the abolition movement would have the tougher road ahead because of intense racism in the country and the feeling among many Americans that blacks were inferior and thus not capable of becoming free and full citizens of the United States; others might say women would have it more difficult because of society's view that they were the weaker sex as well as its long-held beliefs that women belonged at home not out in the world.

Chapter 3, Section 3
GEOGRAPHY APPLICATION

Responses may vary on the inferential questions. Sample responses are given for those.

1. 10

2. The east/west borders of the United States officially became the Atlantic and the Pacific oceans.

3. New Mexico

4. Arizona

5. California, Nevada, Utah, Arizona, New Mexico, and Texas

6. $25 million

7. Statehood was usually influenced by population. (Nevada, an exception, was brought into the Union during the Civil War.) Some of the states had resources and climates that attracted large numbers of settlers, while others did not. The discovery of gold in California, for example, attracted many people to the area. States such as Arizona and New Mexico had few resources and little land for traditional farming, which may have discouraged prospective settlers in the 19th century.

Chapter 3, Section 2
OUTLINE MAP

1. Seminole and Creek

2. Shawnee and Seneca

3. North Carolina, Georgia, Alabama, and Tennessee

4. 3; Georgia, Alabama, Tennessee, Kentucky, Illinois, Missouri, and Arkansas Territory

5. The former group was forced into the unorganized territories (that became Iowa and Kansas) while the latter group was sent to the Indian Territory of present-day Oklahoma.

6. about 1,000 miles

Chapter 3, Section 2
PRIMARY SOURCE

The Hayne-Webster Debates
Possible responses:

1. Both Hayne and Webster believed in the preservation of the Union. Hayne believed that the states should judge for themselves whether laws passed by Congress were constitutional, whereas Webster believed that the federal government and the Constitution had ultimate sovereignty.

2. Informally assess students' public speaking skills and their discussion about the speeches. You may want to point out to students that Webster spoke for four hours—without notes—and that before 1860 the closing paragraphs of the excerpt were memorized by hun-dreds of thousands of schoolboys.

Chapter 3, Section 3
PRIMARY SOURCE

James K. Polk's Speech on War with Mexico

1. Reasons for war: The end of diplomatic and economic relations; disagreement with Mexico over the annexation of Texas; the Texas-Mexico boundary dispute; and the skirmish between Mexican and American soldiers near the Rio Grande

2. The United States attempted to reestablish diplomatic relations by sending an envoy to Mexico and responded with restraint when Mexico committed wrongs against the United States.

3. Some students may point out that Polk's emotional appeals to American's patriotism helped sway Congress. Others may say that Polk's inclusion in his message of the April 25 attack on American soldiers by Mexican forces convinced Congress to vote for war.

Chapter 3, Section 5
PRIMARY SOURCE

Propaganda Images
Possible responses:

1. According to the "before" picture, a person living in Africa was an uncivilized savage, without clothing or shelter, who lived by hunting with a spear.

2. According to the "after" picture, slavery "civilized" Africans and gave them an opportunity to enjoy the finer things in life, such as clothing, art, and the right to visit their master's furnished home.

3. "After" images might include the harsh realities of plantation life such as being punished by an overseer, working long hours doing back-breaking work, or living in squalid slave quarters.

Chapter 3, Section 5
PRIMARY SOURCE

The Seneca Falls "Declaration of Sentiments"

1. Students may point out that women have gained the right to vote, to own property, and to keep their own wages. They may also point out that married couples are now more equal partners with similar legal rights. On the other hand, students may note that although women have more educational and employment opportunities today than ever before, they still frequently do not earn equal pay for equal work.

2. Students may point out that both documents formally declared natural rights; the Declaration of Independence specifically addresses the rights of all men, whereas the Declaration of Sentiments addresses the rights of women. They may also mention specific similarities in form and language.

Chapter 3, Section 3
LITERATURE SELECTION

Roughing It

1. Informally assess the clarity and accuracy of each group's presentation. You may want to encourage students to use visual aids such as charts, maps, photographs, and diagrams.

2. Diagrams will vary. Some effects might include a rapid increase in population, an increase in crime, an increase in accidental deaths, and the rapid growth of mining towns.

3. Students might choose stories such as "The Outcasts of Poker Flat" by Harte or "All Gold Canyon" by London. Encourage students to read their essays to the class.

Chapter 3, Section 1
AMERICAN LIVES

Tecumseh
Possible responses:

1. By learning European history, he might have learned how many British and Americans thought and reacted to situations.

2. Tecumseh's plan was a good idea: only by joining together could the Native Americans have enough power to resist further advances.

3. Tecumseh was such a respected leader and powerful speaker that he probably would have been able to persuade his followers to wait instead of attacking too soon.

Chapter 3, Section 2
AMERICAN LIVES

Henry Clay

Possible responses:

1. Virginia was a more settled society—and power was in the hands of established families. Kentucky, more open at the time, would give Clay more opportunities.

2. Clay's economic plans were based on the idea of extending American national power and benefiting all sections, not just the West. In his political compromises, too, he tried to find solutions that would appeal to all regions.

3. Because Kentucky was neither a Northern nor a Southern state, Clay was not identified with either extreme position.

Chapter 4, Section 1
GUIDED READING

A. Possible answers:

1. Proslavery forces: proposed a new and more effective fugitive slave law

   Antislavery forces: provided that California be admitted as a free state

2. Proslavery forces: held that alleged fugitives were not entitled to a trial by jury; stipulated that anyone convicted of helping a fugitive was subject to a fine and imprisonment

3. Antislavery forces: provided a means of escape for fugitive slaves

4. Proslavery forces: established popular sovereignty in the new territories

5. Antislavery forces: believed that the spread of slavery threatened the free labor system; opposed slavery on moral grounds

6. Proslavery forces: held that being on free territory did not make a slave

free; appeared to permit and even guarantee the extension of slavery

7. Antislavery forces: was an attempt to ignite a general slave uprising

8. Antislavery forces: Lincoln opposed expansion of slavery and felt that slavery was morally wrong.

B. Possible answers:

   Harriet Beecher Stowe: the abolitionist author of *Uncle Tom's Cabin*, which stirred strong reactions from both Northerners and Southerners

   Lincoln-Douglas debates: widened the split in the Democratic Party; brought Lincoln to the nation's attention

   Jefferson Davis: the president of the Confederate States of America

Chapter 4, Section 2
GUIDED READING

A. Possible answers:

1. The Civil War begins.

2. Lincoln's desire to win the war; the need to appease abolitionists; the need to harm the Confederate war effort (slaves were being used to aid the war effort in the South)

3. African Americans make up nearly 10 percent of the Northern army; African-American soldiers serve bravely; African-American soldiers suffer discrimination.

4. Food prices skyrocket, and inflation rises 7,000 percent.

B. Possible answers

   Bull Run: Northern army defeated in the first battle of the Civil War; led Lincoln to step up enlistments

   Antietam: bloodiest single-day battle in American history; Northern army prevented the Confederates from attacking Washington

   Robert E. Lee: brilliant Southern general who drove McClellan away from Richmond

Chapter 4, Section 3
GUIDED READING

Possible answers:

1. It broke the charm of Robert E. Lee's invincibility; shattered Southern morale.

2. Abraham Lincoln helped the nation realize that it was a single nation, not just a collection of states.

3. Strategy: to destroy Lee's army in Virginia while Sherman raided Georgia

   Tactics: attack constantly; engage in total war (against civilians, as well as the military)

4. Goal: to destroy the will of Southerners to fight

   Tactics: engage in total war; destroy civilian property

5. John Wilkes Booth assassinated President Lincoln five days after Lee surrendered to Grant at Appomattox.

6. Political changes: increased the federal government's authority and power; gave the national government more control over individual citizens

   Economic changes: The Northern economy boomed, while the Southern economy was devastated; wrecked most of the South's industry and ruined much of its farmland.

7. The Thirteenth Amendment abolished slavery in the United States.

Chapter 4, Section 4
GUIDED READING

A. Possible answers:

1. Political Problems: Radical Republicans oppose Johnson's Reconstruction plan; Johnson continues to block Reconstruction; money crises plague the Grant administration; Hayes makes a political deal with Southern Democrats during the national election of 1876

   Responses: Congress shifts control of the Reconstruction process from the executive branch to the legislature; Congress impeaches Johnson; economic crisis draw the attention of voters and politicians away from Reconstruction; Reconstruction ends

2. Economic Problems: Southern farms are ruined, and the region's population is devastated; the planter class wants to restore the plantation system

   Responses: Republican governments begin public works programs to repair the physical damage and to provide social services; landowners initiate the sharecropping system

3. Social Problems: African Americans in the South deal with freedom; Ku Klux Klan terrorizes Republicans and African Americans

Responses: African Americans move to towns and cities to find new work. They also seek an education, build churches and schools, and take an active role in the political process; Congress passes a series of Enforcement Acts

B. Possible answers:

Fifteenth Amendment: gave African-American men the vote

scalawag: a white Southerner who joined the Republican Party

carpetbagger: a white Northerner who moved to the South during Reconstruction for either honorable or unscrupulous reasons

sharecropping: a system in which workers farmed land belonging to another in exchange for a share of the crop

Rutherford B. Hayes: Republican president elected in 1876; struck deal with Democrats, which effectively ended Reconstruction in the South

Chapter 4
BUILDING VOCABULARY

A.

1. Fort Sumter

2. Radicals

3. Underground Railroad

4. Gettysburg

5. scalawags

6. conscription

B.

1. f	6. b
2. h	7. i
3. a	8. c
4. j	9. d
5. g	10. e

C. Answers will vary

Chapter 4, Section 1
SKILLBUILDER PRACTICE

Emancipation Proclamation: year—1863; significance—freed all slaves under Confederate control, injected a moral purpose to the Northern cause, boosted the Union's moral; Thirteenth Amendment: year —1865 (ratified); significance—abolished slavery in the United States; Civil Rights Act: year—1866; significance—gave African Americans citizenship and forbade states from passing black codes; Fourteenth Amendment: year—1866; significance—guaranteed rights of citizenship to African Americans; Reconstruction Act: year—1867; significance—divided the Confederacy into military districts and required them to ratify the Fourteenth Amendment before reentering the Union; Fifteenth Amendment: year—1870 (ratified); significance—guaranteed African American males the right to vote

1. Possible Answer: Name of Battle, Date, Site, Victor, Significance

2. Possible Answer: Name of President, Party, Dates of Presidency, Notable Accomplishments

Chapter 4, Section 1
SKILLBUILDER PRACTICE

Time lines will vary; possible entries:

May 4–June 9 Jackson wins battles with Union troops in Shenandoah Valley, then joins Lee's army.

May 31 Confed. forces attack Union troops in Battle of Fair Oaks, then retreat to Richmond.

June 1 Lee takes command of Army of Northern Virginia.

June 25–July 1 Union and Confed. troops clash in Seven Days' Battles.

June 27 Battle of Gaines Mill

June 29 Battle of Savage's Station

Chapter 4, Section 4
SKILLBUILDER PRACTICE

Possible responses:

1. The butchers didn't get their businesses back; state and local governments could legally limit the rights of former slaves.

2. Northerners became discouraged about Reconstruction because its

provisions couldn't be enforced, and they eventually gave up on it. Southern Democrats then took control and cut back on the rights of freed black men.

3. During one decade, the late 1860s to the 1870s, the Supreme Court interpreted a citizen's protected rights so narrowly that politicians and others were able to take away many of the civil liberties that African Americans had gained during Reconstruction. This example demonstrates the power to interpret the "law of the land," with which the Court influences lawmakers from Congress to State legislatures and town and county councils and the behavior of all citizens. Also, by determining what will and will not be tolerated, the Court influences law enforcement.

Chapter 4, Section 1
RETEACHING ACTIVITIES

1. d	5. c
2. a	6. a
3. b	7. b
4. c	8. d

Chapter 4, Section 2
RETEACHING ACTIVITIES

1. blockade

2. enlistments

3. David Farragut, New Orleans, split in half

4. Robert E. Lee, Richmond

5. George McClellan

6. Union

7. discrimination

8. prisons

9. expanded, devastated

10. Red Cross

Chapter 4, Section 3
RETEACHING ACTIVITIES

A.

Chancellorsville—May 1863; South; led to the death of General Stonewall Jackson; Gettysburg—July1863; North; Lee gave up any hope of invading the North again; Vicksburg—May-July 1863; North; the Union achieved its goal of cutting the Confederacy in two; Richmond—April 1865; North; prompted the South to surrender

B.

1. T

2. As a result of the war, the North's economy boomed, while the economy of the South slumped.

3. T

4. The Thirteenth Amendment abolished slavery in the United States.

Chapter 4, Section 4
RETEACHING ACTIVITIES

A.

Johnson—pardoned most Confederates who swore an allegiance to the Union; states could form new state governments and send representatives to Congress as soon as 10 percent of its population took an oath of allegiance.

Radicals—divided the Confederacy into five military districts and required states to give African-American men the right to vote and to ratify the Fourteenth Amendment before rejoining the Union.

B.

1. African American

2. Redemption

3. Amnesty Act

4. Panic of 1873

5. Ten-Percent Plan

Chapter 4, Section 1
GEOGRAPHY APPLICATION

Responses may vary on the inferential questions. Sample responses are given for those.

1. Virginia, Maryland, North Carolina, South Carolina, Texas, Kentucky, Georgia, Florida, Alabama, Mississippi, Louisiana, Arkansas, Missouri, and Tennessee

2. Oregon, California, Minnesota, and Iowa

3. These three states were on the very edge of the Confederacy. They had many fewer slaves than the rest of the Southern states. They must have

seen that there were disadvantages to siding with the Southern states.

4. Texas, Georgia, Florida, North Carolina, Louisiana, and Virginia

5. New York, California, Texas, Florida, Georgia, and Illinois

6. Possible answer: The South was their home and had been for as long as they or their families had been in America, and they did not wish to leave it. Also, they might have thought that things would be different for them in the South after the war.

Chapter 4, Section 2
OUTLINE MAP

1. 11

2. Missouri, Kentucky, West Virginia, Maryland, and Delaware; West Virginia

3. Mississippi River

4. For the Confederacy, about 2,000 miles; for the Union, about 600 miles; Possible response: With more than three times the coastline, the Confederacy could have easily received the supplies from Europe and elsewhere that might have made its war effort more successful.

5. Possible response: It left the core of the Confederacy completely surrounded by Union forces.

Chapter 4, Section 1
PRIMARY SOURCE

The Lincoln-Douglas Debates

1. Informally assess students' re-creation of the debates. Before they begin, you may want to point out that the Lincoln-Douglas debates mixed political drama with the atmosphere of a festival, including horse-drawn floats and banners. Encourage students to deliver their speeches in Lincoln's or Douglas's characteristic manner as described on page 163 of their textbooks.

2. Students may base their slogans on: Douglas's belief in popular sovereignty or the right of residents of a territory to vote for or against slavery; Lincoln's conviction that slavery was morally, socially, and politically wrong.

Chapter 4, Section 2
PRIMARY SOURCE

The Emancipation Proclamation

1. Before students complete their charts, you may want to have them review pages 172–173 in their textbooks.

Possible moral effects: Freed slaves under Confederate control; generated public support for the Union

Possible military effects: Allowed free blacks to enlist in Union army; turned the Civil War into a war against slavery; increased the Confederacy's resolve to fight against the Union; gave Union soldiers renewed incentive for fighting.

2. Informally assess students' paraphrases on the accuracy of the information as well as on the clarity of expression.

Chapter 4, Section 3
PRIMARY SOURCE

On the Burning of Columbia, South Carolina

1. Sherman placed the blame on Confederate General Wade Hampton and the weather. Sherman claimed that after Hampton ordered all cotton burned before the Union troops arrived, the smoldering fires were "rekindled by the wind" and raged out of control.

2. According to the report, Union soldiers saved houses and protected families. Sherman also mentions that some soldiers who were not on duty or who had been prisoners of war may have helped spread the fire after it started.

3. Some students will believe the report because Sherman's account is so detailed and because his explanation is plausible. On the other hand, some students may question the reliability of the report given Sherman's belief in total war and his destructive march through Georgia. After your students have finished their discussion, tell them that Sherman himself admitted much of his report was imaginative and that historians have not yet resolved the question of responsibility.

Chapter 4, Section 4
PRIMARY SOURCE

An Inquiry on the Condition of the South

1. Students should list specific questions related to violence, intimidation, and economic pressure aimed against African Americans and against the whites who offered their support.

2. Informally assess students' role-playing. You might encourage them to role-play additional testimony gathered by the Joint Select Committee and to videotape the proceedings.

3. Students might mention such witnesses as a former slave, a white landowner, or a member of a vigilante group. They might also mention specific witnesses, such as William Beverly Nash, who are quoted in their textbooks.

Chapter 4, Section 4
LITERATURE SELECTION

Jubilee

1. Possible responses:

   Positive aspects: the opportunity to get an education, to attend church, to own a home, to live as a family, to work for wages, to travel freely without a pass

   Negative aspects: discrimination, intimidation by whites, Ku Klux Klan violence

2. Informally assess students' diary entries on the basis of creativity and historical merit. You may want to encourage students to share their entries with the class.

3. Students' stories will vary but should accurately answer the questions who, what, where, when, why, and how. Before students begin writing, you may want to provide them with models of stories from a local or national newspaper.

Chapter 4, Section 1
AMERICAN LIVES

Harriet Tubman

Possible responses:

1. The escape route was called the Underground Railroad because the escapees had to travel in complete secrecy.

2. Slave owners placed a high reward on Tubman because in helping slaves escape to freedom she was undermining the system of slavery.

3. Tubman had to lead the slaves to Canada because passage of the Fugitive Slave Law made it too dangerous for them to live even in the North. They were subject to being seized and sent back South.

Chapter 4, Section 4
AMERICAN LIVES

Thaddeus Stevens

Possible responses:

1. Stevens worked his entire public life to help the poor and the deprived.

2. Stevens spoke harshly of opponents, often calling them names. Such tactics are unlikely to convince others to change their minds in a debate.

3. Stevens's life was not a failure. He helped to overthrow slavery and tried to provide for African Americans' full rights.